INTERSECTIONALITY IN HIGHER EDUCATION

An Action Guide for Change

Edited by
Arun Verma

First published in Great Britain in 2026 by

Policy Press, an imprint of
Bristol University Press
University of Bristol
1–9 Old Park Hill
Bristol
BS2 8BB
UK
t: +44 (0)117 374 6645
e: bup-info@bristol.ac.uk

Details of international sales and distribution partners are available at policy.bristoluniversitypress.co.uk

DOI: 10.51952/9781447377115

British Library Cataloguing in Publication Data
A catalogue record for this book is available from the British Library

ISBN 978-1-4473-7709-2 paperback
ISBN 978-1-4473-7710-8 ePub
ISBN 978-1-4473-7711-5 ePDF

Cover design: Bristol University Press
Front cover image: iStock/Andrey Danilovich
Bristol University Press and Policy Press use environmentally responsible print partners.
Printed and bound in Great Britain by CPI Group (UK) Ltd, Croydon, CR0 4YY

Bristol University Press' authorised representative in the European Union is: Easy Access System Europe, Mustamäe tee 50, 10621 Tallinn, Estonia,
Email: gpsr.requests@easproject.com

For the next generations, I hope this book serves to help ensure you don't experience the intersectional injustices we did in pursuit of a higher education.

Contents

List of figures and tables

Figures

Tables

Notes on contributors

Ashlee Christoffersen

Postdoctoral Researcher, York University (Canada)

A Banting Postdoctoral Researcher in the Department of Politics and Centre for Feminist Research at York University (Canada), Honorary Fellow at the University of Edinburgh, and Equality Research Consultant, Ashlee's areas of specialism include equity, intersectionality, NGOs, intersectional research methodology, inequalities relating to race, ethnicity, gender and gender identity, sexual orientation, equality policy, and inequalities in higher and further education. She holds a BA in Political Science and Women's Studies (Simon Fraser University, Canada), an MA in Gender Studies (SOAS, University of London), and a PhD in Social Policy (University of Edinburgh, funded by the UK Economic and Social Research Council). Prior to completing her PhD, she held research and practitioner roles at equity-seeking NGOs including the Equality Challenge Unit (now Advance HE) and centred (a London-based LGBTQ+ community development organisation). She is also an elected member of the Steering Committee of the European Consortium for Political Research Standing Group on Gender and Politics.

Kevin Guyan

Chancellor's Fellow, University of Edinburgh

Kevin is a writer and researcher whose work explores the intersection of data and identity, with a particular focus on data practices that engage LGBTQ+ communities in the UK. He is the author of *Rainbow Trap: Queer Lives, Classifications and the Dangers of Inclusion* (Bloomsbury Academic, 2025) and *Queer Data: Using Gender, Sex and Sexuality Data for Action* (Bloomsbury Academic, 2022). Across both books, Kevin examines how the design and management of gender, sex, and sexuality categories impact LGBTQ+ communities in policy, law, and data. Kevin works as a Chancellor's Fellow at the University of Edinburgh and is director of the Gender + Sexuality Data Lab.

Dave Thomas
Associate Professor, Royal College of Art
Dr Dave S.P. Thomas is an Associate Professor at the Royal College of Art. He is also a Senior Fellow of the Higher Education Academy (SFHEA), with over two decades of experience in leadership, management, teaching, and research in the educational sector as well as private and public sector organisations globally. Dave is an Occupational Therapist (remit in social justice) and Public Health Specialist. He is a Board member of the Royal College of Occupational Therapists in England, a member of the Health and Care Professions Council Diversity and Inclusion Forum, and a member of the Office for Students' (OfS) Blended Learning Review Panel. He is also an Associate Consultant at Advance HE, specialising in inclusive leadership, equality, diversity, and inclusion.

Iwi Ugiagbe-Green
Professor, Manchester Metropolitan University
Iwi has worked in higher education since 2000. Her first ten years were in a range of financial administration and accounting roles before transitioning to academia in 2010. Since then, she has delivered sustained educational excellence in higher education and established a track record for successfully leading innovative, impactful strategic projects that enhance student opportunity, experience, and outcomes. She is recognised nationally and internationally as an intentionally inclusive leader, whose praxis is rooted in Ubuntu ('I am, because we are'). Iwi describes herself as an academic activist; a positive agitator who is unapologetic in her commitment to student success. Intersectionality provides a relational anchor that grounds all of the equity work that she undertakes. She is very proud and grateful to have been recently promoted to Professor of Equity in Education and is the 84th Black woman Professor in the UK. She was awarded a National Teaching Fellowship in 2025.

Arun Verma

Professor of Practice, University of London

Professor Verma is a leading figure in implementing and integrating intersectionality in systems, policy and programmes, both nationally and internationally. He is a Head of Inclusion at the University of London and Fellow of the RSA. He completed his doctorate exploring intersectionality in healthcare students' learning, retention and success. He has led the integration and embedding of intersectionality and anti-racist practice in local government commissioning, national and global programmes, policy development, practice and implementation. He has been granted a number of awards facilitating his impact, including receiving a Doctor of Laws (*honoris causa*) from the University of Dundee (2024). He also holds a number of board roles across the public sector, including universities and funders, allowing him to facilitate critical conversations about inclusion, intersectionality, and impact within the sector. His edited collection *Anti-racism in Higher Education: An Action Guide for Change* is accelerating action for inclusion in higher education.

Acknowledgements

This book could not have been possible without the contributing authors, who I would like to express thanks for contributing incredible expertise and thought leadership about integrating intersectionality into higher education.

I thank my husband Sebastian, who has been standing with me in solidarity and has been a source of creative inspiration in the development of this second book, in life, love, and my work.

I would like to thank my parents and sisters, my niece Rhea, and my nephew Nathan, for reminding me of the value of family connectedness. I would like to give thanks to my friendships for sharing experiences that have been a continuous source of love and joy.

Preface

Arun Verma

This edited book was written with individuals who have contributed greatly to the knowledge and action of intersectionality, and as the editor, I am deeply grateful for their time and partnership in this work. We are a community of experts who have taken different perspectives to shed light on the ways in which we can integrate intersectionality into higher education. This book invites you on a journey, starting by grounding intersectionality in its roots and history. The author of Chapter Two, titled 'Positioning intersectionality', begins this journey by explaining where intersectionality has come from, contextualising it in anti-racist analysis. It is here we gain a deeper insight into how intersectionality, while not necessarily invented in the 1980s, emerged to capture the ways in which systems and society refused to see how inequalities intersected long before this time.

Intersectionality was initially utilised to broaden the narrow frame that exists in legislative and policy frameworks. Chapter Three, titled 'Intersectionality in policy', provides a critical commentary on the ways in which intersectionality can offer a novel perspective on higher education policy to close the gaps for those experiencing intersecting oppression. In this chapter, the authors encourage the reader to reimagine designing higher education policies with intersectionality at the heart and what this could mean for students, academics, and professional staff.

The role of data is intrinsic to understanding intersectionality as a structural issue. It is also critical in the development of policies and evaluating intersectional interventions in higher education. In Chapter Four, titled 'An intersectional approach to data', the author extends our thinking beyond data binaries, boxes, and boundaries using an intersectional lens. The author then leads us through case studies to bring to life the ways in which intersectional data can embrace complexity and challenge the equality and identity siloes that serve to separate rather than unite us. These silos can also make it difficult to know what impact and success truly are when putting intersectionality into practice in higher education.

In Chapter Five, titled 'Implementation, impact, and intersectionality', the authors demonstrate a variety of frameworks and tools to help the reader design, develop, and measure the success of intersectional interventions, policies, or initiatives. However, it is noted that case studies are scarce, presenting a challenge to those putting intersectionality into higher education policy and practice. Further case studies are needed to demonstrate the value of an intersectional approach. The editor and authors invite the reader to utilise our framework to better capture case studies that can help universities put intersectionality into practice and better serve our purpose and communities.

Throughout this book, the authors explore the different ways intersectionality can be embedded in higher education. In Chapter Six, I share a commentary on what intersectionality looks like on the horizon to help guide contributions to knowledge, action, and impact. I then reflect on my expertise and conversations with key actors, and articulate that intersectionality can be seen on three horizons: continuing to build knowledge, putting intersectionality into action, and measuring impact. Universities are uniquely best placed to be able to generate knowledge, deliver action, and measure impact in the same system that they operate in. In Chapter Seven, the author provides a critical summary of the vehicles that keep intersectionality moving forward and contribute to these horizons while embracing community, truth, and creativity. The assertion here is that universities are not serving communities that lead only single-issue lives, and that integrating intersectionality can better enable them to meet the needs of the whole community – this change becomes an act of hope that is the core underpinning principle of the book.

1

Introduction

Arun Verma

When I talk about intersectionality, I refer to it as a metaphor, theory, and prism that is not solely an academic endeavour or a pursuit of passion. Intersectionality is a theory that has deep meaning to help connect our humanity to the systems that fail and marginalise us. This book acknowledges and celebrates intersectionality as the result of the contributions of Black women scholar-activists. It is through their voices that intersectionality, as we talk about it today and throughout this book, has been embraced by communities across the world personally, professionally, and academically. In my own experience, it is a lens that helped guide me and encouraged reflection on spaces, places, and experiences that had led me to question my place in this world. I recognise that intersectionality is often contained in academia, but I will now tell you my personal journey to intersectionality and why it has become central to my argument that universities should be authentically and unapologetically inclusive.

I want to share a story of me, the editor and one of the contributing authors of this book. Let me take you back to the early 1990s in the United Kingdom. I grew up in a beautiful part of London. It was a different political context then. There was no social media or internet, but new technologies like mobile phones had started to emerge. I lived in a neighbourhood where there was a sense of community. I remember the milkman used to bring fresh milk in glass bottles, and we never needed the security cameras that we have on our front doors now. This was a peaceful suburban town, and it felt good.

As I grew up in this environment, I thought I was happy. Materially and environmentally, everything was great and I remember enjoying helping my parents out in their shop on some days after school. However, I didn't necessarily feel that I fit in at home, at school, or in the area. When I was much younger, I existed on the margins where joy and fear would intersect, leading me to juggle emotions that were overwhelming. I grew up in a family that celebrated British and Indian culture and community, and while I was at school I battled with bullying and trying to figure out my own identities. During my adolescent years, I felt displaced and like I didn't belong. I didn't fit in anywhere as a 'young, gay, brown, British, Indian, Hindu son and man'. This led to shame and a constant state of conflict within myself. It was during this time I learnt to disconnect my mind from my body, which I later realised was a dualism. This turbulent and internal conflict triggered me to hate my skin and my body. This is because it did not match up with the identity and cultural boxes that society had prescribed to me. I did not fit in with the environment I was navigating at the time, which was often white, middle-class, and heteronormative. I was none of those things, so how could I ever fit in and feel happy? I became afraid to be my true self. I remained quiet and struggled to find my voice. I chose not to speak up. I chose to hide and focus on self-preservation rather than expressing myself.

After experiencing harassment at school, I wanted and probably needed to get help. I found a service in the local area that was LGBTQIA+-inclusive. It was here where I had my first contact with a counsellor. But it was in secret; I told no one because I was terrified of coming out about who I was to the world. I lived a double life, and the toll was dear. I got into trouble because I told myself and my body that I did not care. This continued throughout my teenage years, until I left for travelling and then later to embark on my first degree.

When I got to university, I started to experience liberation and to connect with people who shared some of the experiences that I had. For a while, it was great, but it was in queer spaces where I experienced unexpected racist abuse. I did not know what to do with these experiences. They ranged from verbal harassment to physical assault. I was knocked back to my childhood, falling back to the margins and feeling like I should not have existed anywhere. I was reliving my displacement and finding that I had nowhere to belong.

It did not take long for my anxiety to capitalise on this, and I quickly learnt to embrace self-hatred. I hated my skin. I hated my body again. I hated my mind. It took me several years of deep reflection and counselling to learn to exist and find a more sustainable intrinsic source of happiness and joy; these intersecting margins, these hidden cracks in the system I kept falling through. Falling through the cracks led to bouts of isolation and sadness throughout my adolescence. I recall a good friend telling me to go to a monastery for rest and recuperation during a time when I was struggling at university. I travelled on the boat during a stormy evening to the Isle of Wight. I got off and lugged my suitcase and backpack over a muddy path to find sanctuary. I remember knocking on a small old wooden door. A St Benedictine monk welcomed me and showed me to my room. I stayed there for a few days. I sat with the monks in the library discussing philosophy and theology. I helped clean the corridors to pay for my room. I listened to the readings during dinner. I took mindful walks on paths through the gardens to the sea. That time taught me to just exist and experience myself, both the joyful and the fearful emotional parts of who I am. I was able to fully appreciate that if I wanted to experience joy and love, I needed to accept my intersectional self.

This acceptance was not easy – and it is an ongoing process, particularly as it is compounded by intersecting inequalities. After my stay at the monastery, I learnt that my intersectional discomfort was slowly becoming a source of strength and a journey to self-love. I realised at this time that I did not want to fit into a box anymore.

It was during my pursuit of postgraduate research when I came into contact with the word 'intersectionality'. I was at my desk in the doctoral students' office in the first month of my doctoral journey. I was handed a pile of articles and books to read before I got stuck into the research. One of the articles that I was told to read first, published in the 2010s, used the term 'intersectionality'.

There was a spark that happened when I read the article, and it piqued my curiosity. The authors of this particular paper claimed ownership of the theory. However, as my curiosity grew, I felt the need to explore more deeply what 'intersectionality' really meant and where it came from. It was at this time in postgraduate research that I started to become consumed by this concept of intersectionality. When I think back to that time, I recall the early mornings and late evenings in the library and the doctoral students' office, annotating and reading about theories of inequality, professionalism, and the conception of intersectionality. Of course, I came across the famed article written by Crenshaw (1989), coining the term intersectionality, which I read time and time again. I sifted through the references of Crenshaw's paper and worked my way through them. I continued my discovery and researched and read countless articles about intersectionality, racial justice, colonialism, among many other subjects. I watched videos and listened to talks that referenced intersectionality. The more I engaged with this concept in my academic research, the more I noticed I was learning about myself and my place in the world. I deeply reflected on the materials I engaged with and realised that my experience of marginalisation was a result of existing between categories that society and systems had prescribed to me. These were boxes I never chose, nor did I have any interest in 'fitting in'. I learnt that because of who I am, a queer, brown-skinned, British Indian, man, I would find myself in the cracks of the system, failing to find the support I needed. When I was at university, student networks played a key role in helping me think about where I could fit in. But the communities that I sought support and solidarity within only existed in silos so I still did not know where or how to exist. The LGBT+ student network was run by white peers and the Hindu society was only for those who were heterosexual, and I didn't have headspace to be part of both. I ended up participating more in the LGBT+ group, feeling like I had to put a piece of who I was to the side.

Intersectionality broadened the frame of how I saw myself. It became a theory of hope and joy for me. It provided me with a prism that said I did not have to be part of a system of silos because that did not fit the human experience or the dynamicity of identities. I began to believe that I was not broken and could see myself taking steps to let go of my self-hatred. I would read late into the night about intersectionality with questions in my head posed to the literature. It felt as though I was in conversation with the authors of these papers – authors who kindly invited me to embark on a pathway to self-care and love.

Intersectionality was brought to light by Black women scholar-activists, who are all referenced throughout this book and in my previous edited collection *Anti-Racism in Higher Education: An Action Guide for Change* (Verma, 2022). It was their stories, contribution to knowledge, activism, and power that have allowed for the centring of the voices and experiences of Black women, and later for the centring of some of the most marginalised communities in the world. The more I read about intersectionality, the more I went back, and I discovered how intersectionality was driven by activism to eradicate racial and social injustice. The purpose of intersectionality is not to put one intersectional community ahead of any other community. It is not designed to pit communities against each other. Instead, it is a theory that aims to provide justice to the most intersectionally oppressed groups and to develop transformational change for a more socially just society.

Recently, the theory of intersectionality has become a little more watered down. I was in a conversation with a budding equality and inclusion consultant, who wanted to speak to me about things to consider when setting up as an independent consultant. When we did introductions, I explained that my specialism is in 'intersectionality'. They replied with the statement, 'well, everyone is intersectional, aren't they?' Their statement poses three assertions. The first is that no one person is one thing, the notion that 'everyone is intersectional' means that people experience life and inequality in a way that is shaped by their intersecting characteristics and identities. The second point is that whilst 'everyone is intersectional', the premise of intersectionality centres the voices of those experiencing intersectional oppression to create a system change. The third assertion is related to the way in which there is a minimising of the value of intersectionality as only about identities. It is much more than that. It is here where intersectionality leads to both transformative action and joyfulness in order to challenge racial and equality hierarchies and critically question the ways in which certain social categorisations are perhaps not fit for purpose in our society. The critical issue here in that person's response is they neglected and excluded the excellence of Black women who propelled this concept into the mainstream, which allowed us to tell a more authentic story of inequality and demand more.

Journey to joy

Before I embarked on an intersectionality journey, I was practicing acts of unkindness to myself. This was a result of my displacement and my lack of self-esteem, value, and worth. Reading the words written by Kimberlé Crenshaw, Angela Davis, and bell hooks, imagining and rehearsing my conversations with these authors' words, I realised this was not just an academic exercise. This was deeply personal, emotional, and soulful. I remember when I read *All About Love* by bell hooks and was met with a quote which became a turning point in my life:

> Self-love cannot flourish in isolation. It is no easy task to be self-loving. Simple axioms that make self-love sound easy only make matters worse. It leaves many people wondering why, if it is so easy, they continue to be trapped by feelings of low self-esteem or self-hatred. Using a working definition of love that tells us it is the action we take on behalf of our own or another's spiritual growth provides us with a beginning blueprint for working on the issue of self-love.
>
> (hooks, 2000 p.54)

When I read this quote, it helped me to understand how difficult it is to love yourself when you are trying so hard to fit into a box. It is when we break down these boxes and categories that we are able to give ourselves permission to love ourselves in our entirety, including the mess. The more I engaged in, participated in, and spoke about joy, the more my interactions and engagement with people started to change. It felt as though I went through a slow transformation towards loving myself. When I embraced a loving mindset, I saw people, society, and systems with a more appreciative lens.

However, I realise that the world and higher education are not always so forgiving. The stories that I engaged with, which people shared with me, showed me the level of suffering Black and minority ethnic women were experiencing every day. The widening gaps in the retention and success of students and staff in universities are shocking to this day. This journey to joy does not overwrite these inequalities, but it is the addressing of these inequalities and their transformation into love that can make the change happen. I resolved that my act of disruption would be to insert as much compassion and joy into the spaces I moved through to challenge the status quo of racism, ableism, sexism, misogynoir, and transphobia (to name only some) that is often the norm in universities. When I receive social media messages and emails, I kindly respond to as many as I can so those individuals are not ignored (except for the junk and phishing messages of course). When someone is talking to me, I ensure I face the individual with my body to show them I am actively listening and paying attention to their words and respecting the space I am privileged to be invited in to. I ask people how they are managing their wellbeing and self-care on a regular basis. I ensure I compliment and support wherever possible and always reply to someone with 'yes, and' to enable dialogue and human connection. I don't do all of these things perfectly, but my intention is to bring joyfulness to a world that is increasingly unforgiving and filled with injustice. This, I feel, is the essence of integrating intersectionality into practice.

As I continued to read about intersectionality, it was not just the theoretical prism or analytical framework that encouraged me to keep telling the story of inequality. It was the recognition that embracing intersectionality is the only way we are going to achieve outcomes that create a dignified, fair, and respectful society and culture in higher education. When reading this book, I invite you to recognise that by integrating intersectionality into all aspects of the higher education system, we are more likely to create spaces where society and systems empower us to practice self-love, compassion, and joy. When I talk about joy, I mean the ability for people to work together to create a fair, thriving, and respectful society where no one is adversely impacted by intersectional inequality.

Why intersectionality in higher education?

Phrases and statements about 'doing' intersectionality have been posed to me through a variety of talks, workshops, groups, and meetings in recent years, with many requests from delegates and leaders asking me to define intersectionality within the higher education context and share how it can be put into practice. Having delivered a great number of keynotes and talks in various formats over the last few years, these questions became so frequent, I resolved that this book would respond to those years of questions and support the higher education sector in putting intersectionality into action. I am privileged to have connected and collaborated with individuals who employ intersectionality as experts in their universities and beyond to provide a guiding light to integrating intersectionality into the higher education system. It is through conversations with these individuals that I hear from people who want universities to succeed and be places where joyfulness, innovation, and success are embraced and felt.

The role of higher education in society and the world is to create space where knowledge, research, and innovation can collide, as well as to help inform and bring society closer together to support our collective advancement. The idea that knowledge is power is a principle that is threaded through our education systems. It is this pedagogical principle that we equip our learners with to find their power and navigate the complexity and challenges of the world. The origin story of higher education as we know it today stems from medieval schools known as '*studia generalia*', which were typically attended by theologians, monks, and clerks from the Global North. These institutions promoted educational free movement for students across Europe to learn, exchange, and joyfully collide in research and scholarship (Şenocak, 2012). While this romantic idea of the university existed and inclusivity was felt by communities in the Global North and Europe, higher education was also complicit in perpetuating global inequalities and atrocities, stemming from colonial and imperial efforts across the world (see, for example, Gani and Marshall, 2022; Mullen, 2021; Ziadah, 2025).

Over the course of colonial and imperialist efforts, members of communities from across the world were moved to the Global North. Universities became more exclusive, with higher education places typically held for elite white men with promising potential careers in the Church, who were taught about societal systems and structures of law and theology. However, with the introduction of elementary education and new philosophical and scientific thinking, the range of disciplines and subjects taught in higher education was broadened to serve and offer support to a modernising and changing society (Fayaz, 2020). Throughout all the changes the university sector has adapted to, higher education has played a transformative role in advancing and serving society. Universities now often focus on issues like 'civic engagement' and 'social purpose' in an effort to demonstrate their worth actively in the community. World leaders, great and not so great, have typically been through a university process that has enabled them to navigate the challenges faced by both their nations and the world. Our higher education sector has produced ideas, theories, and discovered solutions to challenges far ahead of its time. For example, our collective and international success in overcoming the COVID-19 pandemic was a result of operating, unknowingly intersectionally, to rapidly protect people from a virus that killed so many across the world. These medical, educational, and societal solutions stemmed from global university partnerships. The greatest artists, thinkers, and theorists have debated, discussed, and negotiated ideas in universities, which have gone on to shift global conversations on critical issues ranging from mental health and wellbeing to sustainability and theories of leadership and inequality. Universities are and have always been powerhouses in producing knowledge that influences research and everyday conversations.

Higher education institutions are also experts in multi-tasking. They engage prospective students from across the world to explore and discover ways of contributing to society, while producing knowledge and innovation that enables society to be informed and learn to critically engage with information. Universities are also critical mirrors to policies, economies, and political narratives that influence people's lives. This is a considerable evolution from the days in which universities were known as '*studia generalia*' and only served the few. However, universities are increasingly in a corporate drive to serve mass markets, for both financial sustainability and prestige, rather than focused on developing educational excellence, future leaders, and joyful disruptors. I hear stories from impassioned colleagues where their institutions arguably dehumanise students with their language, boxing them in as 'financially active' and 'customers'. Or other stories where the performance of staff is monitored by only using one economic and financial metric – another box. The concern here is whether this language of boxes enables people to achieve and produce educational excellence, which is surely central to a university's purpose.

More often than not the universities that exist across the Global North do not represent the intersectional diversity of the students they are trying to engage, often relying on 'excellence' and 'saviourism' as corporate or marketing values. These values used to work in a time when Global North education was thriving. As the world changes and social media widens its reach, people know more about universities and their role than they did before. The question remains whether universities have adapted enough to meet the needs of an intersectional world. I propose that a university that has truly integrated intersectionality would solve some of its most pressing challenges, including creating joyful and thriving institutional cultures, overcoming financial barriers, empowering freedom of speech, and actualising student success. My question to you is, who is willing to lead the way?

Thinking ahead

Hope is what brought this book to life, and the hope of this book is for higher education institutions to become better at sustaining themselves in an intersectional world. We produced this book with the intention, hope, and optimism that if we put intersectionality into practice in universities, our higher education community will truly achieve joy, liberation, and excellence. The role of this book is to enable a deeper knowledge and understanding of intersectionality. This is to ensure that the story of inequality that has enabled this theory, metaphor, and prism to come to light is told and embedded into areas where change can be most effective. The book draws out questions to enable you, the reader, to critically reflect on the themes and systematic issues that have been highlighted by myself and the contributing authors. This is an opportunity to deepen your learning and think about what is possible when putting intersectionality into practice both as an individual and within institutions

References

Crenshaw, K.W. (1989). Demarginalizing the intersection of race and sex: A Black feminist critique of antidiscrimination doctrine, feminist theory and antiracist politics. *University of Chicago Legal Forum*, 139. Available at: https://scholarship.law.columbia.edu/faculty_scholarship/3007 [Accessed 6 April 2026].

Fayaz, Z. (2020). The purpose of universities: From the Middle Ages to the age of Covid. The Brand Education. Available at: https://thebrandeducation.com/blog/the-purpose-of-universities-from-the-middle-ages-to-the-age-of-covid/ [Accessed 22 July 2025].

Gani, J.K. and Marshall, J. (2022). The impact of colonialism on policy and knowledge production in International Relations. *International Affairs*, 98(1), pp.5–22. https://doi.org/10.1093/ia/iiab226.

hooks, b. (2000). *All about love: New visions.* London: William Morrow and Company.

Mullen, C.A. (2021). Pedagogies for Decolonizing Education in Theory and Practice. In C.A. Mullen, ed. Handbook of Social Justice Interventions in Education. Springer International Handbooks of Education. Springer, Cham. https://doi.org/10.1007/978-3-030-35858-7_91

Şenocak, N. (2012). The Franciscan *studium generale*: A new interpretation. *Rencontres de philosophie médiévale*, pp.221–236. https://doi.org/10.1484/m.rpm-eb.1.100978.

Verma, A., ed. (2022). *Anti-racism in higher education: an action guide for change.* Bristol: Policy Press.

Ziadah, R. (2025). Genocide, neutrality, and the university sector. *The Sociological Review*, 73(2), pp.241–248. https://doi.org/10.1177/00380261251321336.

2

Positioning intersectionality

Iwi Ugiagbe-Green

Origin story

They say, 'A labour of love, is no labour at all'. As an academic activist, constantly labouring to make 'good trouble' (Lewis, 2018), the opportunity to write a chapter for this wonderful edited book by Professor Arun Verma, who I hold in the highest regard, was warmly accepted with deep gratitude. It is my belief that many people do not really understand the complex nature of intersectionality. As such, I have really struggled to balance the simultaneous intellectual challenge of theorising and positioning it within scholarship, whilst also aiming to provide an accessible, practical analysis of its positioning . My weary heart witnesses the appropriation and co-option of intersectionality to advance an anti-woke agenda (yes, in universities too), hence my need to call it out and challenge it.

I start by making my own positionality very clear. I am a Black woman academic activist whose practice is anchored by the South African philosophy of Ubuntu ('I am because we are'). I am a global citizen of the world whose practice is also influenced and shaped by Black feminism. To me, intersectionality is not only a conceptualisation, a lens, a framework, and/or tool of analysis. Intersectionality provides fundamental sense-making of my positioning by others (and that which is subsequently internalised) and my response and resistance to that in a world that sees me as different, an 'alien' in some lands. More than anything, my understanding of the antecedents of intersectionality as rooted in Black feminism and its appropriation and co-option make me hold more firmly onto the belief expressed by the ever-wonderful bell hooks (2000) that, 'if any female feels she need anything beyond herself to legitimate and validate her existence, she is already giving away her power to be self-defining, her agency' (p.95). That is, that to thrive as a Black woman in higher education and the world, is to know I need not be anything beyond myself.

Intersectionality names a phenomenon (the unique configuration of discrimination faced by Black women) that existed long before its conceptualisation. Black feminism movements provided the basis on which the named expression, coined by Crenshaw, was given to spotlight that white bodies receive the benefits of systemic protections not offered to Black bodies. This is not a new phenomenon revealed by intersectionality, but by naming it and attaching it to bodied identity and experience Crenshaw (1989) brought it to the mainstream. Cooper (2016) explains that intersectionality has become a key analytical framework used in different fields to discuss issues not only pertaining to race and sex but now to class, gender, and sexuality. Its widespread adoption across many different contexts means it is applied in ways beyond its original conception. To understand this assertion is to understand its origins and the importance of Black women and Black feminism to its original conceptualisation.

W.E.B. Du Bois (1903) theorised about the mutual reinforcement of race, class, and culture in social stratification, although he did not explicitly include gender. In 1977, the Combahee River Collective, a group of Black queer socialist feminists, addressed the 'interlocking oppressions of racism, sexism, and heteronormativity'. (Encyclopædia Britannica, 2025). There were many under-resourced Black women movements and brilliant Black feminist scholars who leveraged their power, unique insights, and experiences to create new knowledge about inequalities, shaping the later conceptualisation of intersectionality. In 1969, American civil rights activist Frances Beal wrote *Double Jeopardy: To Be Black and Female*. In 1995, Michele Wallace in her essay 'Anger in isolation: a Black feminist's search for sisterhood' explained how Black women feminists are stranded and at the bottom of society (Wallace, 1995). In *Ain't I a Woman: Black Women and Feminism* (1981), bell hooks critically examined how the legacy of slavery has shaped contemporary perceptions of Black womanhood and how both the feminist and civil rights movements have often marginalised Black women's experiences. These Black feminism texts are foundational to what is now known as 'intersectionality'. It is important to acknowledge that integral and central to the foundational conceptualisation of intersectionality is the oppression of women. However, the oppression of women needs to be understood beyond boundary gendered analysis.

Professor Kimberlé Crenshaw explained that it was her studies in law that led her to coin 'intersectionality', now a mainstream term. She cited three central legal cases that dealt with the issues of both racial discrimination and sex discrimination: *DeGraffenreid v. General Motors*, *Moore v. Hughes Helicopter, Inc.*, and *Payne v. Travenol.* In each case, Crenshaw argued that the court's narrow view of discrimination was a prime example of the 'conceptual limitations of … single-issue analyses' regarding how the law considers both racism and sexism (Vox, 2019). She explained that the courts would say that if you don't experience racism in the same way as a (Black) man does or sexism in the same way a white woman does, then you haven't been discriminated against (Equal Rights Review, 2016). Crenshaw developed the term by applying the lens to Black women's experiences in law, starkly surfacing the systemic inequality embedded in the mechanisms of the law experienced by Black women. As Sir William Blackstone in 1893 explains, the law 'is that rule of action which is prescribed by some superior and which the inferior is bound to obey' (Vol 1, Section 2). Crenshaw's work demonstrated the inferiority of Black women in the eyes of the law.

Her 1989 paper, 'Demarginalizing the intersection of race and sex: A Black feminist critique of antidiscrimination doctrine, feminist theory and antiracist politics', Crenshaw explained how 'women of color' face discriminations that are not addressed by either feminist or anti-racism movements. The 'whitening of intersectionality' (Bilge, 2014) has diluted or misapplied the intersectionality emergent from Black feminism. However, Black feminism is not about Black feminists, in the same way that white feminism is not about white women who are feminists. White feminism is a form of feminism that has 'whiteness', a nebulous concept that Garner (2007) describes as 'a racialised as well as classed boundary marker' (p.59), at its core. White feminism offers boundary gender analysis only and often positions Black feminism as divisive; with some questioning why or how Black and white feminism is even a thing. Black feminism offers a multi-axis (for example, sexism, classism, racism) framework, which extends beyond the boundary of gender analysis, offering understanding of the compounding and unique configurations of inequity that affect Black women, but also trans women, refugee women, Gypsy, Roma and Traveller women, and other marginalised women groups. What Crenshaw (1991) exposes so convincingly, is that to view identities of 'women of color' from a single axis framework that uses boundary gender analysis only serves 'to 'relegate(s) them to a location that resists telling' (p.1242). Intersectionality enables the counter-narratives and stories of marginalised people to be told, but it has lost its focus as a framework rooted in Black feminism to understand systemic inequality and become a 'catch-all means to discuss any form of intersecting identity' (Daramy and Dumangane Jr., 2025, p.89).

It is the impact of structural inequality, told in the stories and counter-stories of those who are marginalised and minoritised, that is exposed by intersectionality.

Systemic positioning of intersectionality

Social science concepts like intersectionality, which are interdependent on social systems and structures and anchored by observable phenomenon, will inevitably further develop and evolve over time. To understand why this happens is to understand that intersectionality, as an evolving theory, is underpinned by the post-positivist philosophy of critical realism (Bhaskar, 1998).

Critical realism explains that there are structures and mechanisms that exist, outside of the social constructions we may not be able to observe, that shape social phenomena. Critical realism provides the philosophical grounding that positions intersectionality as a theory, a framework, and a lens that enables us to better understand (and in some cases predict) lived experiences of people with different intersecting characteristics. An exploration of discrimination in social structures in critical realist terms exists across three levels: the causal, actual, and empirical (Werkmeister Rozas, 2022). At the causal level are the mechanisms and logics – for example, hegemony (power structures that you cannot see) – that influence and impact lived experience of interactions within social systems. These reciprocal interactions at the actual level (things in material form; for example, events, experiences) shape our knowledge and understandings of the world. This means that we socially construct unseen mechanisms – for example, patriarchy – that shape actual experiences – for example, discrimination, racism – and these can be observed at the empirical level. Intersectionality is a lens that exposes the impact of what bell hooks (1994) called the 'imperialist white supremacist capitalist patriarchy' (p.248); an interlocking system of power, capitalism, and patriarchy that functions together to maintain social structures.

Critical race theory (Matsuda et al., 1993; Bell, 1995) is a theory relating to critical realism and observes that it is power systems, mechanisms, and logics by design that perpetuate and sustain racism. Therefore, intersectionality applies a racialised lens to empirically observe and explain individuals' experiences within social systems, adopting an 'ontology of persons' (Bhaskar, 2020). Its grounding in critical realism enables empirical observation of the impact of causal systemic racism – for example, capitalism – and can help with understanding racism in the context of individuals lived experiences. Empirical studies, where intersectionality is used to observe this phenomenon, show that we can reasonably predict which racialised groups will suffer racial inequalities compared with those who are not. Bell (1980) did this in his book, *Race, Racism and American Law*, in which he illustrated how laws systematically disempower Black people. Bell exposes the routine function and operation of the law as a system that disproportionately adversely impacts on the rights and justice of Black people. Critical race realism is emergent from critical legal studies and synthesises critical realism and critical race theory. It is considered a race-based, systematic critique of legal reasoning and legal institutions (Delgado and Stefancic, 2000).

That intersectionality was birthed from Black feminist thought and that law is the domain in which its conceptualisation is situated and continues to evolve is very important to remember and, in some ways, sadly ironic. After all, this concept that tells us so much about systemic inequality originated in the discipline of law, from which important fields such as critical race realism have developed. Sadly ironic because shouldn't the law be about freedom, justice, and peace for all?

Systemic and political intersectionality

Presently, there is a political discourse proposing we recentre the law as the touchstone of fairness. Calls to recentre the rule of law is largely in response to what has been referred to by some as the dominance of 'woke ideology'. Woke ideology has been labelled by some as unfair, arbitrarily favouring specific groups because of beliefs, with little robust 'evidence' or 'data' to support the 'business case' to do so. This ongoing pushback against the 'woke' challenge to the colonial matrix, is to ensure that the system maintains the status quo. People who depoliticise the law to suggest it is the material mechanism by which to deliver fairness in society have a rooted belief that the state and its laws maintain fairness in world order. As such, the 'moral economy' (an order of morals that considers welfare, humanitarianism, and civil society; Götz, 2015) is ascribed to law – law of course, being the original domain, in which intersectionality was conceptualised.

The contestation to law as the moral economy is supported by empirical evidence of the realities of interactions between people in the system: the stop and search and incarceration rates of different racialised groups of people, the relative death rates of racialised people in police custody, and the continued dehumanisation of Black women by the police. A recent pertinent and harrowing example of this is the 2021 case of two serving police officers (Deniz Jaffer and Jamie Lewis) in the UK, who shared photographs with other police officers of the mutilated bodies of two Black murdered sisters, Nicole Smallman and Bibaa Henry. In court, they expressed that this was done as 'chit chat and to 'be funny' (BBC, 2022). The oppression of Black bodies at the 'moral hand' of the law does not end, even in death.

Political ideologies are not only held by individuals within social structures, but they are organised, powerful doctrines of an influential collective, determining how society should work. Capitalism is an example of a political ideology, intrinsically linked to class structures through its economic principles and the way it organises society (Wright, 1997). There are deep-rooted links between capitalism and social structures that determine social stratification. Hall et al. (1978) explain that 'race is the modality through which class is lived' (p.394). They explain that class and race are intertwined and that the experiences of people from different class positionings are mediated by their racialisation.

Again, to understand the importance of class on intersectionality, is to understand the emergence of class structures as a material impact of colonial logics. Land occupation, and its commodification and commercialisation, created class hierarchy (Ghertner and Lake, 2021). Reproduction of those class hierarchies was enabled through laws that gave power to settlers to own land, displace Indigenous peoples, and sustain intergenerational wealth from the economic gains that came with corporatising and extracting from the land. These activities push out people with low economic capital out of 'high value land' in order that settlers and owners of the land can continue to profit (Adebisi, 2023). Changes in demography and associated population growth, aging populations, and migration patterns can impact economic structures too. The capitalist value proposition, of economic benefit at the expense of sustainability of the land, is driven and maintained by these colonial logics and is what drives and sustains social class structures and their associated racialised hierarchies. For example, we have seen governments of countries in Africa adopt colonial logics to exploit and extract from the land in pursuit of profit, while Indigenous peoples have been decentred and marginalised (Ubink, 2008).

In socialist (rather than capitalist) structures, where commodification of land and production is owned collectively by the state or society (Harvey, 2003), the colonial logics of social systems operate differently. Both capitalist and socialist economic systems have their historical roots in colonialism and imperialism (Achcar, 2021). Post-colonial states sometimes adopted socialism to move away from colonial economic systems (Msindo, 2018). However, political ideologies associated with socialist systems that adopt, for example, state intervention to redistribute wealth and provide collective welfare only shift the positioning and mapping of the colonial matrix. Fundamentally, the organisation of social structures does not dislodge the colonial logics that operate as mechanisms to perpetuate racialised hierarchies.

The intentions and actions of agents within social systems that ensure mechanisms respond and react to changes to maintain the 'world order' are informed by knowledge systems that we cannot see. The organisation of economic systems, reflective of the capitalist value proposition, remains a mechanism by which to operate colonial logics. Intersectionality as a lens for empiricism –for example, as a site of data analysis – means we can observe the material impacts of interactions within these socio-political economic structures. However, it is the epistemic systems, which shape values, ideologies, and habitus and that are critical to understanding why intersectionality as a theory can predict the material impact of the colonial matrix on specific groups, that cannot be observed. Intersectionality in and of itself does not provide the understanding of why it is conceived, perceived, and intended that the 'world order' should be and is maintained through racialised social structures; it just shows us that it is. It is theories such as critical race theory and critical race realism that provide this understanding.

Justice has become the dominant currency in which we frame our aspirations for a better world (Macklem, 2020). The way of the world is not fair to all persons, and the push for a better world is necessary because people experience the world and its social structures inequitably. The racialisation of people within social structures is used to malign, dehumanise, marginalise, and minoritise people who are perceived as not embodying ideals of whiteness. However, it is not only the perceived proximity to whiteness of a physical and embodied racialised body that influences racial identity. The ontology of people in racialised terms, goes beyond the idea of a fixed identity. Fanon (1952) explains in *Black Skin, White Masks* that we are fixed by our own appearance at the surface, but it is the schema that sits behind this – the stories, metaphors, and images – that constructs the relationship between the body and social structures. Bodies are used as a site of 'the biological trace' (Hall, 1997) of socio-cultural differences, utilised as a visual signifier of racial difference. In racialised systems of difference, it is not only our bodies that provide the reality of race; colonialism, religion, cultural habits, and so on are variously enrolled to differentiate some bodies from others (Swanton, 2010). Grosfoguel (2016) states: 'The intersectional entanglement between class, sexual, gender or national/colonial oppressions that exist in the zone of non-being are … qualitatively distinct from the ways these oppressions are lived and articulated in the zone of being' (p. 12).

The reflexive and interpersonal occupations of bodies that are racialised mean that intersectionality can provide a lens to see and understand which racial markers are used to differentiate and separate but also unify embodiments of whiteness. Some racial markers used to do so are visual ('hair, skin and bone'; Du Bois, 1897) and not separated from the physical body. There are others – for example, religion and faith –that may not be embodied physically and instead be internalised or hidden. Intersectionality spotlights difference through constructed identities based on racial markers but also reveals to us how these markers are used politically to homogenise, marginalise, and minoritise people who are 'othered' in their interactions. Social constructions of the relationships between racialised bodies and social structures are stories of relations of difference. These stories of difference are shared stories across racialised and gendered lines. They are emotive stories of pain, joy, oppression, liberation, shame, pride, challenge, resistance, power. Ahmed (2004) evokes the term 'affective economies' to argue that emotions do not reside in a subject but rather circulate in relations of difference, whereby what is moved and what moves is the effect of affective intensities and energies. The very real impact of racialisation, a socially constructed and politically driven act of division, is emotive. Grosz (2005) reaffirms this notion of immanence of the reality of being a racialised body – for instance, the ontology of the body and 'the conditions under which bodies are enculturated, psychologized, given identity, historical location, and agency' (p.2).

Systemic power and intersectionality

I hope to have convinced you of why the system and embodiment of whiteness and racialisation is fundamental to understanding intersectionality. There is a function, an intent to the action and conditioning of racialising bodies that is rooted in power, dominance, conformity, and maintaining whiteness.

Race is of course socially constructed. Contrary to general understandings, its conceptualisation is not fixed or only associated with racialised bodies; it is a power mechanism that operates through relations and connections among material, affective, and conceptual elements that might include skin colour, segregation, colonialism, oppression, law, language, and migration. These elements are entangled in processes of differentiation that take an indeterminate direction each time (Swanton, 2010). To understand discrimination inflicted on people in racialised systems (and therefore to understand intersectionality), is to recognise the function of race as a technology (Lentin, 2021). In conceptualising race as technology, our understanding of race and racism as concepts that exceed the binary logics of fixed identities dominating conventional understandings of what race and racism are, is important. Instead, our understanding leads us to focus instead on what race and racism do (Swanton, 2010). The function and intention of race and racism as a technology is to produce, reproduce, and maintain white supremacy at both local and global scale (Lentin, 2021). The 'affective formation', or the emotions and feelings associated with race as technology (Mejia LaPerle, 2021), influence actions that enable stratified social racialised systems to operate and sustain the dominance of specific racialised groups.

As a technology, race and racism format perceptions; exclusion, fear, hatred, suspicion of raced bodies that are not racialised as white are formed. As a technology, it does the work in shaping perceptions, narratives, values, and beliefs associated with the social construction of race. The construction of race is part of the epistemic system, a knowledge system that determines ways of being and knowing. We cannot see this system but use intersectionality to empirically observe its material impacts. Empirical analysis reveals that race is not a fixed concept. Racial classification is borne of epistemic systems, oscillating between biology, phenomenology, anthropology, religion, and culture. Its function is to maintain social systems that distribute wealth, power, capital, and knowledge across (racially) stratified society structures.

Creating racially stratified groups of division and control is a necessary constant to maintaining 'world order' across time and space. Race as a technology mediates, distorts, adapts, and reconfigures the basis on which people are racialised, marginalised, and minoritised to achieve 'world order'. As a technology, it flexes and adapts to changes within social structures to perpetuate its strength in shape shifting. Race seeks to differentiate, to classify, to organise, to segregate, to discriminate, and does so through affective systems.

The spaces of interconnectedness within and between social structures in society, such as the state, institutions, community groups, families, are where social interactions happen. This creates an ecosystem (Folke et al., 2010), where social structures are connected to physical structures; land and various social roles and interactions within and across social structures contribute to the overall functioning of society. These material structures did not just appear; they were and continue to be created and organised with intention. Intention is built on values, motivations, beliefs, knowledge systems, and actions with a desired outcome. Social structures organised as institutions are funded with capital, status, and roles, with a range of desired outcomes. Their operations and the interactions that take place within them are bound together with regulations, laws, norms, and values that people internalise, embody, and action. Organised power within institutions, that is both claimed and distributed through social stratification, is used to maintain 'world order' (Kissinger, 2014). This involves the ways in which the world is organised and viewed to achieve stability and progress (Acharya, 2023).

Social stratification as a structural process has its roots in land settlement or settler occupation, modes of production, and resource availability and distribution (Grusky, 2001). The infrastructure is formally organised by socio-political ideologies and mechanisms that determine how resources are produced, distributed, and consumed. These systems shape social hierarchies and relationships between different social groups across them. So, the formation: the intentional design of these systems and continued development and sustained power of their associated social structures is rooted in capitalist systems (and the distribution of these resources) that sustain and perpetuate racial hierarchies. This is conceptualised by Quijano (2000) as the 'colonial matrix'.

Mills (1997) wrote in *The Racial Contract* that 'white supremacy is the unnamed political system that has made the modern world what it is today' (p.1) – in other words, the 'world order'. Political ideologies can shape, reshape, and be shaped by colonial logics – the ordering and world-making frameworks, founded on racial and gender difference, through which the unequal relations of dispossession and exploitation within extractive capitalism are governed, perpetuated, and tethered (Gómez-Barris, 2017; Murrey and Jackson, 2020). Colonial logics enable 'the system' to find a way to sustain racial stratification and hierarchy in society. There are clear examples of this from history where, for example, after the 13th Amendment to the US Constitution to 'officially abolish slavery' was made in 1865 (National Archives, 1865), the Jim Crow laws that enforced racial segregation and economic disparities were brought in in the late 19th century until the mid 20th century to maintain white supremacy and the economic exploitation of Black Americans. Later, in South Africa, apartheid was used to ensure that Black South Africans (Indigenous persons of the land) were confined to low wage labour occupations and denied access to housing, education, and healthcare. In the UK after the Second World War, racially minoritised people (the so called, 'Windrush Generation') from the Commonwealth countries were invited to rebuild Britain only for laws that removed their citizenship and associated rights to housing, education, healthcare to be subsequently enacted to position them as illegal immigrants.

My own maternal grandparents from Jamaica were encouraged to uproot their life and family and leave their homeland to come the 'motherland'. They were promised a life of prosperity and opportunity in return for helping to rebuild the English economy in the aftermath of the Second World War. Instead, the systemic oppression that they and many of their friends endured on arriving to rebuild the 'motherland' is an unwelcome legacy of displacement, othering, and ostracisation, resulting in generational barriers to opportunity and long-term financial struggle.

But as bell hooks tells us:

> to be in the margins is to be part of the whole, but not the main body … the sense of wholeness, impressed upon our consciousness by the structure of our daily lives, provided us an oppositional world view – a mode of seeing unknown to most of our oppressors that sustained us, aided our struggle to transcend poverty and despair, strengthened our sense of self.
>
> (hooks, 1984, p.341)

As the daughter of immigrants born in England, I have learnt how to navigate and unapologetically resist against a system that tries to position me to give away my agency, my power, and legitimise and validate my existence. Progressing through academia as a student, then as a graduate and academic, has been a life-shaping contradiction of deep pain and deep joy. The words cited above by the great bell hooks are a faithful representation of my daily life in academia.

As such, in many ways the next section on the three facets of intersectionality in the higher education context explains a world in which, I, a Black woman academic have become whole.

Structural intersectionality in higher education

Intersectionality affirms that discrimination and oppression, as part of modes of existence, are not restricted to the relational or the interactional. Inequality is not simply limited to how people make you feel. That it is a site, a location, a specific and unique configuration situated on the colonial matrix is important. To understand it as a site of oppression, which is located relative to hegemonic structures within a system, means that to address issues of inequality requires action beyond the relational, the interactional. It is important to understand that inequality extends beyond the relational and is also about the spatial and the systemic. The geography, politics, and positionality of intersectionality is critical to acknowledging how enablers such as functions of mechanisms (for example, the technology of race) in social systems (for example, institutions) maintain world order. Grosfoguel

(2016) explains that the westernised, modern university has spent over 500 years reinforcing and re-enacting colonial logics that maintain its sites of inequity.

Universities uphold and reaffirm structures of power and wealth. Contemporary practices normalise the ways of university systems (Keval and Wright, 2021) as exclusionary and institutionally racist, operating politics of the plantation (Stewart et al., 2025). Universities reward and support the 'ideological subservience of the plantation'. (Stewart, cited in Tuitt et al., 2018). This ideological positioning is not only evidenced by structures such as the 'snowy peak' of leadership in higher education; it is also evident in the relational – in the experiences of racially minoritised staff who are less likely to progress and be promoted and more likely to be subjected to bullying and harassment from colleagues (UCU, 2016)

Intersectionality recognises the unique barriers to accessing and succeeding in the sector (Crenshaw, 1989). The higher education sector has responded to addressing this issue with gender equity schemes and aspirational charter awards (for example, Athena Swan and Race Equality Charter) that recognise an institution's commitment to equality, diversity, and inclusion (EDI). These charters are considered by some as apparatus of colonialism (Strongman, 2007). They are used by universities to provide a signalling effect of an institution's commitment to equity and equality. Yet institutions that operate systems that perpetuate harm and disadvantage to minoritised groups and reaffirm the dominance of specific groups – for example, through adopting the practice of plantation politics (Stewart, et al., 2025) – are still awarded these charters.

Political intersectionality in higher education

Universities operate in a neoliberal socio-political environment. Neoliberalism is the discourse that justifies global capitalism as the dominant socio-economic system and seeks to extend capitalism to all spheres of life (Morley et al., 2017). As a result, activities and interactions within the social structures of universities are driven by quasi-marketisation policies. Success in higher education is largely framed using economic based outcomes (Ugiagbe-Green et al., 2025).

Intersectionality is applied as an ontological project (Hancock, 2007) to try and understand the impact of interactions of students within university structures based on award or graduate outcomes. Consequently, it can be used to reshape higher education policy to make accommodations within existing policy more inclusive or equitable – for example, through the introduction of contextual admissions as part of the widening access and participation agenda. It is gaining much traction in the policy space through the increasing use of intersectionality reporting. However, there are many issues associated with the conceptualisation of intersectionality reporting and its problematic use for this purpose in higher education (see Ugiagbe-Green and Ernsting, 2022, where we highlight that systemic oppression cannot be measured by statistical methods through analysis of single-point social locations). Intersectionality provides a lens of analysis that exposes the interlocking, transient, reconstitutive forms of inequality experienced by people situated across a multi-axis colonial matrix.

Intersectionality reporting in higher education assumes that by aggregating single-point social locations of inequality, we can measure inequality to benchmark outcomes, and then 'level up' through targeted interventions. Targeted interventions seek to redress differential outcomes through tackling issues that lead to differential outcomes. This is done through providing enhanced support and opportunity to specific targeted student groups. As such, intersectionality in universities is perceived by some to be a problematic attempt to systemise equality of outcome. Engineering outcomes to meet fixed quotas or targets is unlawful. The law does not permit positive action by companies to employ practices in order to determine outcomes based on race or any other characteristic. To be clear, I do not propose that universities are using intersectionality to standardise outcomes. What I do propose is that it is being used to better understand differential outcomes and take action to address the inequalities that are surfaced by the intersectional analysis. The use of intersectionality to influence or address differential outcomes is deemed to be problematic by those who popularise the idea of 'reverse discrimination'. Resistance to equity work as 'reverse discrimination' by some is rooted in a view that universities operate meritocratic systems, where hard work is rewarded by success. The myth of meritocracy is particularly prevalent in universities. This myth is based on the idea that individuals succeed purely based on talent, intelligence, and effort, without acknowledgement of the role of privilege, opportunity, bias, and systemic inequalities. There are certainly people in higher education who consider intersectionality as a tool that exposes those who do not work hard enough, rather than as a liminal space of inequality.

It is said that 'when you're accustomed to privilege, equality feels like oppression'. As such, intersectionality is also increasingly used by some to malign those who are 'socially disadvantaged' or 'under-resourced,' – so-called disadvantaged students. It is used by some to recentre the proposition that 'All Lives Matter' and insultingly suggest that 'Black Lives Matter' is discriminatory. This is the affective response to equity actions that prioritise the needs of some people over others, with perceptions held that this creates hierarchies of oppression. This negative affective response to equity is rooted in a belief that all social systems are meritocratic, and that targeted support for groups in this way is therefore unfair, undeserved, and in some cases, 'unlawful' benevolence (positive action is perceived as positive discrimination). This position is supported by a belief that the 'cream always rises to the top'. This belief is often taken up by the same people who believe that DEI (diversity, equity and inclusion) stands for 'didn't earn it'.

Relational intersectionality in higher education

The university is a place and space of paradox. Universities are spaces where trailblazing, radical academics challenge hegemony, patriarchy, and whiteness and try to foster decolonial thinking by drawing on 'historiographical constructions of freedom, agency and equality' (Grosfoguel, 2016). Yet universities are also places where the bodies of staff and students are routinely racially minoritised and/or erased in data, in regulatory reporting, and in the sector's framing of success. This routine activity happens in an extractive higher education system in which the emotional labour and tax of leading the work to challenge colonial logics and trying to foster decolonial and praxis thought is rarely acknowledged or rewarded. Most people leading this critical work are racially minoritised people. Rather than being rewarded, racially minoritised people are psychologically gaslighted, isolated, and demeaned when they name the problem (Bhopal and Henderson, 2019, Arday and Mirza, 2018, Rollock, 2012).

In 2021, Professor David Richardson, Vice Chancellor of University of East Anglia and then Chair of Universities UK, stated that 'UK Universities are institutionally racist' (The Guardian, 2021). There was an inevitable backlash from some universities who argued that this was not the case, coupled with decries of unfair generalisations. However, the fact remains that universities are sites of structural, institutional, and behavioural racism.

In academia, intersectionality is often used as a site of analysis to support persuasive arguments highlighting the need to implement interventions to promote equality through gender and/or ethnicity equity. It is also a framing that is used to explain why single-issue initiatives such as Athena Swan (gender equity), introduced by higher education organisation the Equality Challenge Unit (now Advance HE) in 2005, have mainly benefited one group of women (white middle-class women) rather than all women groups (Bhopal and Henderson, 2019). The scheme was intended to serve all women, but it is the dominant group of already well-resourced women in academia who have benefited from the scheme. Intersectionality, as a theory, explains why this is the case. The scheme is rooted in white feminism rather than having a multiple-axes, intersectional approach to its design. Consequently, again it is racially minoritised women who are further marginalised. Conversely, WHEN 100, a professional development programme developed by WHEN, a private UK company, is specifically designed to increase representation of Black women professors in UK academia[1]. In both instances, intersectionality is used as a shared language to understand the need, justification, and outcomes of these schemes.

Here we see that intersectionality is being used to support the view that there is a need for inclusion (particularly at senior leadership levels) in higher education. Central to this proposition is that it is important that diverse groups of people with different intersecting characteristics are represented. It is widely proposed that a sign of the 'system working' is if racially minoritised people 'make it' to the 'snowy peak' of academia. As such, intersectionality can also provide a reference point for us to understand what is valued by systems of whiteness. Value is inherently attached to racialised bodies that are deemed to have assimilated into the system – in other words, the 'model minority' (Yukich, 2013). Model minorities are also perceived to have accomplishments (Hsu, 2015) that give them access to spaces beyond the margins. Keval (2025) refers to these accomplishments as the 'sovereign indicators of winning'. These are the symbols, the stories, and the accomplishments associated with someone 'winning' within the system.

As an accomplished Black woman academic working from the margins within higher education, I often reflect on critical questions about my complicity in a system of whiteness that has recognised and rewarded me. A system that I have both benefited from and try to disrupt. I regularly ask myself: 'have I been given membership to a club to which I should not belong? Am I, as a senior leader working in higher education, absorbed by the effervescence of whiteness? Do sovereign indicators of winning mean that I am I benefiting from colonial logics because I am complicit within the system? What does that complicity mean for my integrity?' Intersectionality holds a mirror up to us all. It provides us with an opportunity to reconcile the acknowledgement of the value we ascribe to sovereign indicators that we pursue, while simultaneously holding strong intrinsic motivations to disrupt the system from which we seek to benefit. Intersectionality shows us that nobody is immune from colonial conditioning.

In universities, there are different mechanisms used by institutions to try and redress colonial conditioning within our universities. These are commonly different formations of equity or equality, diversity, and inclusion roles, functions, and teams (for example, EDI, ED&I, or DEI). The work of EDI teams focuses on the relational – our interactions, relations, intentions, perceptions, navigations of the system rather than a disruption to its structures. The aspiration of many EDI teams in universities is to be 'award-winning' and achieve 'sovereign symbols' of success – for example, charter marks, such as 'Athena Swan, Race Equality Charter' accreditations, described by Strongman (2007) as the apparatus of colonialism.

Inequities are experienced through agentic relations, operationalised through affective systems, and rooted and anchored in the colonial matrix. It is my view that inequality in our universities will not be addressed by making our university communities more diverse, or by creating community spaces where people feel a sense of belonging and mattering (as important as these things are at the agentic relations level within the system). The words of Maya Angelou in her 1973 interview with Bill Moyers are particularly pertinent here: 'You only are free when you realise you belong no place – you belong every place – no place at all' (Moyers, 1973). She reminds us that we only belong to ourselves. The place of our ultimate relational interaction. Our modes of existence are shaped by our ontological and epistemological ways of being and knowing over time and place. Intersectionality affirms that to become whole, is to practice love for oneself rather than believe it is a reward of a meritocratic system. The onto-epistemological philosophy of Ubuntu ('I am, because we are') encourages the practice of love to develop widely within groups, communities, and then societies. Love, therefore, has a revolutionary potential. Love is what has enabled me to thrive in a system in which I believe I belong every place.

Reimagining the university: worlds otherwise

It is with themes of love and hope that I end this chapter. I am forever optimistic, but also realistic about what Derrick Bell explains as the permanence of racism (Bell, 1992).

Nasar Meer in his 2022 book explores the concept of 'cruel optimism' in the context of racial justice. He argues that optimism for racial equality can be counterproductive, as it often normalises social and political outcomes that perpetuate racial disparities (Meer, 2022). A critical question to ask therefore, is given that intersectionality has been co-opted into the mainstream, has it become counterproductive? Crenshaw explains that intersectionality isn't an effort to create the world in an inverted image of what it is now (Vox, 2019). Instead, she explains that the point of intersectionality is to make room 'for more advocacy and remedial practices' to create a more egalitarian system rather than to reproduce hierarchies and dominance (Vox, 2019).

Intersectionality was never intended to be, nor can it be the tool that dismantles the colonial matrix and disrupts the colonial logics that maintain locums of dominance, power, and the politics of positionality in our universities. Universities are a microcosm of society and function in the same way that all social structures do to maintain the status quo. A 'worlds otherwise' (Zibechi, 2024) requires a dismantling of relations of power and conceptions of knowledge, ideologies, and understandings (Maldonado-Torres, 2011).

To reimagine the university requires the roots of intersectionality, its advocacy for an egalitarian system in which all human rights are equal and Black women are not discriminated against, to be disrupted by decolonial thought too. Our very existence as Black women is relative to the world(s) in which we inhabit and is within the context of the colonial matrix. As such, intersectionality provides not only a lens, but a reflective lens, enabling individuals to not only understand the mechanisms of colonial conditioning but also to consider ways in which colonial conditioning can be challenged, redressed, and unlearned.

The start of this chapter explains that intersectionality emerged from Black feminism, which recognises as Audre Lorde explains, 'no such thing as a single-issue struggle, because we do not live single-issue lives' (Lorde, 2012[1982]). The ways in which I am in the world, the view of myself (and others), and my positioning in the world as a Black woman would need to be radically different. My modes of existence would need to shift radically. I have internalised and am socialised by colonial conditioning in my ways of being and interacting with others. Reimagining requires creating entirely new worlds and ways of being. In my own equity work, I value the 'marginal gains' I make through my academic activism as a way of 'disruption' against the system. But what if in thinking there is value in small reforms, this delays or prevents more radical, necessary transformation to dismantle existing power structures and colonial logics? Is approaching my work in this way enabling the system to function its colonial logics? But then, is the dismantling of 500 years of 'epistemic superiority, and psychological, social and embodied racial trauma' (Keval, 2025) even possible? How does the onto-epistemological understanding of self through interactions with others deepen understanding of intersectionality? Can this understanding enable radical change? A 'worlds otherwise' means that lives would need to be determined by a borderless, non-extractive 'free world' far beyond the realities of what we have now. This would require a complete social reordering of systems and a radical reimagining (Walia, 2021).

Intersectionality shows us the reality of who we are and what we are as a society right now. We all occupy fractured, opposing, bordered spaces both within and outside of the university. The unique configurations of inequity experienced by people within racialised systems are not fixed points on the colonial matrix. They are dynamic, shape shifting over time and space, as the technology of race adapts and changes. Intersectionality reveals, whether it be via a lens, prism, framework, tool, site of analysis, or theory, that, in and of itself, it does not provide the healing and liberatory potential of the heart and mind needed to reimagine higher education. My exploration of intersectionality and higher education tells us that universities are not the spaces for this either. Intersectionality provides a way of knowing and of being. A way to understand what it is to be different, to not belong within a system that shape shifts and contorts to ensure you stay in your place. But, the space, the place to which we all belong is to ourselves. It is here, in the spirit of Ubuntu, in the practice of love for ourselves and each other, where we can change not only higher education, but the world.

I end with the words of another amazing Black feminist, Audre Lorde (1984) who says:

> [It] is within our differences that we are both most powerful and most vulnerable, and some of the most difficult tasks of our lives are the claiming of differences and learning to use those differences for bridges rather than as barriers between us. (p.115)

Reflective questions

- As a member of the higher education community, what actions can you implement to help create a more egalitarian system rather than to reproduce hierarchies and dominance?

- What reflections do you have related to 'sovereign indicators of winning,' and whether they are a proxy measure of one's complicity in upholding inequitable systems of power and privilege?
- What actionable pledge can you commit to ensure that you consistently and intentionally treat people for whom you hold bias with care and empathy?

Note

1 https://www.whenequality.org/

References

Acharya, A. (2023). Before the nation-state: Civilizations, world orders, and the origins of global international relations, *The Chinese Journal of International Politics*, 16(3), pp.263–288, https://doi.org/10.1093/cjip/poad011.

Achcar, G. (2021). Colonialism / imperialism / orientalism. In J.-N. Ducange, R. Keucheyan, and S. Roza, eds. *Histoire globale des socialismes XIX-XXIe siècle*. Paris: Presses Universitaires de France, pp.109–122.

Adebisi, F., (2023). *Decolonisation and legal knowledge: Reflections on power and possibility*. Bristol: Bristol University Press.

Ahmed, S. (2004). Affective economies. Social Text, 79(22.2), pp.117–139. Available at: http://muse.jhu.edu/journals/soc/summary/v022/22.2ahmed.html [Accessed 6 April 2026].

Arday, J. and Mirza, H.S. (2018). Dismantling Race in Higher Education. Cham: Springer International Publishing. https://doi.org/10.1007/978-3-319-60261-5.

BBC (2022). Deniz Jaffer: PC who shared photos of dead sisters boasted of cover-up. 8 July 2022. Available at: https://www.bbc.co.uk/news/uk-england-london-62095812 [Accessed 21 April 2025].

Beal, F.M. (1969). *Double Jeopardy: To Be Black and Female*. Detroit: Radical Education Project.

Bell, D.A. (1980). *Race, racism and American law*. 2nd ed. Boston: Little, Brown.

Bell, D.A., (1992). *Faces at the bottom of the well: The permanence of racism*. New York: Basic Books.

Bell, D.A. (1995). Who's afraid of critical race theory? *University of Illinois Law Review*, 1995(4), pp. 893–910.

Bhaskar, R. (1998). Facts and values: Theory and practice. In M. Archer, R. Bhaskar, A. Collier, T. Lawson, and A. Norrie, eds. *Critical realism: Essential readings*. Abingdon: Routledge, pp.409–417.
Bhaskar, R. (2020). Critical realism and the ontology of persons*. *Journal of Critical Realism*, 19(2), pp.113–120. https://doi.org/10.1080/14767430.2020.1734736.
Bhopal, K. and Henderson, H. (2019). Advancing equality in higher education: An exploratory study of the Athena SWAN and Race Equality Charters. British Academy Research Report. Available at: https://www.birmingham.ac.uk/ Documents/college-social-sciences/education/reports/advancingequality-and-higher-education.pdf
Bilge, S. (2014). Whitening intersectionality. Evanescence of race in intersectionality scholarship. In W.D. Hund and A. Lentin, eds. Racism and Sociology. Racism Analysis Yearbook, 5, pp.175–205.
Blackstone. W (1893). *Commentaries on the laws of England in four books. Notes selected from the editions of Archibold, Christian, Coleridge, Chitty, Stewart, Kerr, and others, Barron Field's Analysis, and Additional Notes, and a Life of the Author by George Sharswood. In Two Volumes*. Philadelphia: J.B. Lippincott Co.
Crenshaw, K.W. (1989). Demarginalizing the intersection of race and sex: A Black feminist critique of antidiscrimination doctrine, feminist theory and antiracist politics, *University of Chicago Legal Forum*, 139. Available at: https://scholarship.law.columbia.edu/faculty_scholarship/3007 [Accessed 6 April 2026].
Crenshaw, K. (1991). Mapping the Margins: Intersectionality, Identity Politics, and Violence against Women of Color. *Stanford Law Review*, 43(6), pp. 1241–1299. https://doi.org/10.2307/1229039.
Cooper, B. (2016) 'Intersectionality', in L. Disch and M. Hawkesworth, eds. The Oxford Handbook of Feminist Theory. New York: Oxford University Press, pp. 385–406.
Daramy, F. and Dumangane Jr., C. (2025). "Woke", intersectionality, critical race theory and decolonisation: Misunderstood, misused and weaponized. *Widening Participation and Lifelong Learning*, 27(2), pp.81–103. https://doi.org/10.5456/WPLL.27.2.81.
Delgado, R. and Stefancic, J. (2000). *Critical race theory: The cutting edge*. Philadelphia, PA: Temple University Press.

Du Bois. W.E.B. (1897). The Conservation of Races. The American Negro Academy Occasional Papers, No.2. Washington, D.C.: The American Negro Academy.

Du Bois, W.E.B. (1903). *The souls of Black folk*. Chicago, IL: A. C. McClurg and Company. Available at: http://docsouth.unc.edu/church/duboissouls/menu.html (Accessed 10 October 2006).

Encyclopædia Britannica (2025). Intersectionality. Available at: https://www.britannica.com/topic/intersectionality (Accessed 25 May 2025).

Equal Rights Review (2016). Vol. 16. Available at: https://www.equalrightstrust.org/ertdocumentbank/Intersectionality%20interview%20with%20Kimberle%20Crenshaw%20and%20patricia%20schulz.pdf. [Accessed 8 June 2025].

Fanon, F. (1952). *Black skin, White masks*. New York: Grove Press.

Folke, C., Carpenter, S., Walker, B., Scheffer, M., Chapin, T., and Rockström, J. (2010). Resilience thinking: Integrating resilience, adaptability and transformability. *Ecology and Society*, 15(4). https://www.jstor.org/stable/26268226.

Garner, S. (2007). *Racisms: An Introduction*. London: SAGE Publications.

Ghertner, D.A. and Lake, R.W. (2021). *Land fictions: The commodification of land in city and country*. Ithaca, NY: Cornell University Press.

Gómez-Barris, M. (2017). *The extractive zone: Social ecologies and decolonial perspectives*. Durham, NC: Duke University Press.

Götz, N. (2015). 'Moral economy': Its conceptual history and analytical prospects. *Journal of Global Ethics, 11*(2), pp.147–162. https://doi.org/10.1080/17449626.2015.1054556.

Grosfoguel, R. (2016). What is racism? *Journal of World-Systems Research*, 22(1), pp.9–15.

Grosz E. (2005). *The nick of time: Politics, evolution, and the untimely*. Durham: Duke University Press.

Hall, S., Critcher, C., Jefferson, T., Clarke, J., and Roberts, B. (1978). *Policing the crisis: Mugging, the state, and law and order*. London: Macmillan

Hall, S. (1997). 'Stuart Hall: Race the floating signifier' [online], Available at: https://www.youtube.com/watch?v=PodKki9g2Pw [Accessed 21 April 2026].

Harvey, D. (2003). *The new imperialism*. Oxford: Oxford University Press.

hooks, b. (1981). *Ain't I a Woman: Black Women and Feminism*. Boston, MA: South End Press.

hooks. b (1984). *Feminist Theory: From Margin to Centre*. Boston, MA: South End Press.

hooks, b. (1994). *Outlaw Culture: Resisting Representations*. New York: Routledge.

hooks, b. (2000). *Feminism is for everybody: Passionate politics*. Cambridge, MA: South End Press.

Hsu, M. Y. (2015). *The good immigrants: How the yellow peril became the model minority*. Princeton, NJ: Princeton University Press.

Keval, H., and Wright, T. (2021). Necropolitical constructions of happiness, COVID-19 and higher education. *Critical Studies on Security*, 9(2), pp. 170–173. https://doi.org/10.1080/21624887.2021.1978644.

Keval, H. (2025). *Whiteness, racial trauma, and the university*. London: SAGE Publications.

Kissinger, H. (2014). *World Order*. New York: Penguin Books.

Lentin, A. (2021). Algorithmic racism. In N.B. Thylstrup, D. Agostinho, A. Ring, C. D'Ignazio, and K. Veel, eds. *Uncertain archives: Critical keywords for big data*. Cambridge, MA: The MIT Press, pp.57–64.

Lewis, J. (2018). *John Lewis: Good Trouble* [Documentary film]. Magnolia Pictures; Participant; CNN Films; AGC Studios; TIME Studios

Lorde, A. (1984). Age, Race, Class, and Sex: Women Redefining Difference. In *Sister outsider: Essays and speeches*. Freeman, CA: Crossing Press, pp. 114–123.

Lorde, A. (2012 [1982]). "Learning from the 60s." Address delivered at Harvard University. *Black Past*, 12 August. Available at: https://www.blackpast.org/african-american-history/1982-audre-lorde-learning-60s/ [Accessed 6 April 2026].

Macklem, T. (2020). The price we pay for justice. *Jurisprudence*, 11(3), pp.417–436.

Maldonado-Torres, N. (2011). Thinking through the decolonial turn: Post-continental interventions in theory, philosophy, and critique—an introduction. *Transmodernity: Journal of Peripheral Cultural Production of the Luso-Hispanic World*, 1, pp.1–15. https://doi.org/10.5070/T412011805.

Matsuda, M.J., Lawrence, C.R., Delgado, R., and Crenshaw, K. (1993). *Words that wound: Critical race theory, assaultive speech, and the first amendment.* Boulder, CO: Westview Press.

Meer, N. (2022). *The cruel optimism of racial justice.* Bristol: Bristol University Press.

Mejia LaPerle, C. (2021). *Race and affect in early modern English literature.* Tempe, AZ: Arizona Center for Medieval and Renaissance Studies.

Mills, C.W. (1997). *The Racial Contract.* Ithaca, NY: Cornell University Press.

Moyers, B. (1973). A Conversation with Maya Angelou. [online] Bill Moyers Journal: Original series, Available at: https://billmoyers.com/content/conversation-maya-angelou/ [Accessed 23 April 2026].

Msindo, E. (2018). Postcolonial Africa and the West. In M.S. Shanguhyia and T. Falola, eds. *The Palgrave handbook of African colonial and postcolonial history.* London: Palgrave Macmillan, pp.759–784.

Murrey, A. and Jackson, N. A. (2020). A decolonial critique of the racialized "localwashing" of extraction in Central Africa. *Annals of the American Association of Geographers*, 110(3), pp.917–940. https://doi.org/10.1080/24694452.2019.1638752.

National Archives (1865). 13th Amendment to the U.S. Constitution: Abolition of slavery. Available at: https://www.archives.gov/milestone-documents/13th-amendment [Accessed 20 April 2025].

Quijano, A. (2000). Coloniality of power, Eurocentrism, and Latin America. *Nepantla: Views from South*, 1(3), pp.533–580.

Rollock, N. (2012). The invisibility of race: intersectional reflections on the liminal space of alterity. *Race Ethnicity and Education*, 15(1), pp.65–84. https://doi.org/10.1080/13613324.2012.638864

Stewart, S., Schlabach, K., Romandia, O., and Tuitt, F. (2025). Old tactics in new robes: Plantation politics and the continued pervasiveness of anti-blackness in higher education. *Journal of Diversity in Higher Education*, 18(6), pp. 883–899.

Strongman, R. (2007). The colonial state apparatus of the school: Development, education, and mimicry in Patrick Chamoiseau's "Une Enfance Créole II: Chemin-d'École" and V.S. Naipaul's "Miguel Street." *Journal of West Indian Literature*, 16(1), pp.83–97. http://www.jstor.org/stable/23019724.

Swanton, D. (2010). Sorting bodies: Race, affect, and everyday multiculture in a mill town in northern England. *Environment and Planning A*, 42(10), pp. 2332–2350. https://doi.org/10.1068/a42395.

The Guardian. (2021) UK universities are institutionally racists, says leading vice-chancellor. 28 April 2021. Available at: https://www.theguardian.com/education/2021/apr/28/uk-universities-are-institutionally-racist-says-leading-vice-chancellor [Accessed 21 April 2026].

Tuitt, F., Hayes, C., and Stewart S. (2018). Transforming the classroom at traditionally White institutions to make Black lives matter. *To Improv Acad*, 37(1), pp. 63–76. https://doi.org/10.1002/tia2.20071.

Ubink, J.M., (2008). *In the land of the Chiefs: Customary law, land conflicts, and the role of the state in peri-urban Ghana*. Leiden: Leiden University Press.

UCU (2016). The experiences of Black and Minority Ethnic staff in further and higher education. London: University and College Union.

Ugiagbe-Green, I. and Ernsting, F. (2022). The wicked problem of B(A)ME degree award gaps and systemic racism in our universities. *Frontiers in Sociology*, 7. p. 971923.

Ugiagbe-Green, I. Massey, S., and, Mann, M. (2025). The challenges of measuring work-readiness and evaluating an intervention to address differential outcomes: A critical analysis. In L. Austen and C. McCaig, eds. *Delivering and evaluating participation after access: Higher education in a marketized system*. Emerald Publishing. pp. 155–174.

Vox. (2019). The intersectionality wars. 28 May. https://www.vox.com/the-highlight/2019/5/20/18542843/intersectionality-conservatism-law-race-gender-discrimination [Accessed 8 June 2025].

Walia, H. (2021). *Border and Rule: Global Migration, Capitalism, and the Rise of Racist Nationalism*. New York: Haymarket.

Wallace, M. (1995). Anger in isolation: a Black feminist's search for sisterhood. In B. Guy-Sheftal, ed. *Words of Fire: An Anthology of African-American Feminist Thought*. New York: The New Press, pp. 219–220.

Werkmeister Rozas, L. (2022). Coloniality of power, critical realism and critical consciousness: the three "C" framework. *Journal of Ethnic & Cultural Diversity in Social Work*, 31(3–5), pp.162–172. https://doi.org/10.1080/15313204.2022.2070890.

Wright, E.O. (1997). *Class counts: Comparative studies in class analysis*. Cambridge: Cambridge University Press.

Yukich, C. (2013). Constructing the model immigrant: Movement strategy and immigrant deservingness in the new sanctuary movement. *Social Problems*, 60(3), pp.302–320, https://doi.org/10.1525/sp.2013.60.3.302.

Zibechi, R. (2024). *Constructing worlds otherwise: Societies in movement and anti-colonial paths in Latin America*. Chico, CA: AK Press.

3

Intersectionality in policy

Ashlee Christoffersen and Arun Verma

In this chapter we delve into intersectionality and policy, drawing on a diverse range of literature to identify how intersectionality is being discussed and used in different policy contexts relevant to higher education (HE). The chapter will first establish how intersectionality relates to different policy discussions: higher education policy in the international context; social policy, with education being an essential component of this; HE sector-level policy; and institutional policy. We will explore the ways in which intersectionality is utilised to inform practice and programmes for social purpose and change. The chapter will also draw on the experiences of the authors in implementing intersectionality into practice to bring to life what exists in the literature. We will review current frameworks of intersectionality that shape the policy development, analysis, and implementation lifecycle. This is done to help identify practices, trends, and what is working when utilising intersectionality in the HE policy space, and what impact is intended and can be foreseen.

Intersectionality in higher education policy in an international context

Policy plays a crucial role in helping higher education institutions develop frameworks and guidance to enable accountability, and to help diverse stakeholders make decisions during turbulent times (Ward et al., 2015). Higher education policies both reflect and respond to social, cultural, and political discourses, which directly influence and change the experiences and outcomes of higher education communities (see Klein et al., 2022; Molla, 2020). Specifically, HE policy may serve to increase or decrease intersecting inequities. Deuel (2021) acknowledges the importance of policy, writing that 'since the late 1980s, intergovernmental organisations (IOs) have promoted and shaped globalising higher education policies (Shahjahan, 2012; Rizvi and Lingard, 2010)' (p.310). Institutions such as the Organisation for Economic Co-operation and Development (OECD), the World Bank, and the World Trade Organization (WTO) have influenced education policy at national, regional, and local levels – for example, in reducing public funding for higher education (Altbach and Knight, 2007); adopting managerial governance practices (Marginson, 2011); developing competitive institutional internationalisation practices (van der Wende, 2007); and increasing international student mobility (Courtois, 2018). Deuel (2021) argues that policy is incredibly influential and this further opens a line of inquiry to positively disrupt systems of oppression and inequity (see Jones et al., 2021; Schipper et al., 2020; Salmi and D'Addio, 2020; Wilson et al., 2021).

We recognise that legal, political, and regulatory frameworks can also variously shape and influence higher education policy depending on where institutions are situated in the world (see, for example, Kaiser et al., 2014). Many higher education institutions operate with explicit international agendas, including delivering transnational education (or TNE) and developing global citizenship. These, in theory, compel HE to have culturally sensitive policies that support global collaboration and empower relationships across regions, geopolitical contexts, and even the Global North and South (Pineda and Mishra, 2022). The role of policy is crucial for higher education to enable viable, sustainable, and inclusive systems and societies (see Salmi and D'Addio, 2020; Bagilhole, 2010; Banerjee, 2024). However, there are significant challenges for developing HE policy that survives national socio-political turbulence and emerging technologies (Yonezawa, 2023; Chankseliani et al., 2020; Murtaza and Hui, 2021).

At the European Union level, it has been found that intersectionality is now more frequently referred to in policy discourses on higher education and research. These policy discourses remain dominated by a strong focus on gender, to the exclusion of other inequalities, and they are also often individualistic, to the exclusion of thinking in terms of structural change. Funding requirements have enabled the enactment of sanitised forms of intersectionality, involving a notion of inclusion that can be exclusionary and a notion of diversity that primarily serves institutional branding (Rodrigues, 2025). Policies are largely race evasive and neglect the need for structural change and decolonial transformation (Jaquetto Pereira, 2025). Thus, there has been an increasing call for more authentic intersectional policies focusing on structural and systems level change, and this is particularly pertinent to universities operating in a world market (Eigenmann et al., 2024).

Intersectional social policy

Social policy is 'concerned with the ways societies across the world meet human needs for security, education, work, health and wellbeing. Social policy addresses how states and societies respond to global challenges of social, demographic and economic change, and of poverty, migration and globalisation' (Platt, 2025, n.p.). This subset of policy is critical to transforming geopolitical agendas to proactively eradicate inequalities so as to support a fair, dignified, and respectful distribution of power, resources, and equitability (Browne et al., 2023). Intersectionality is a tool to help with social policy analysis and interventions to tackle inequalities (Williams, 2021). It is often the case that policies have continued to perpetuate equality silos (for example, treating race and gender as separate categories) and separate communities from the structures and systems they navigate (Qureshi, 2022), as has been observed in HE (Douglas Oloyede et al., 2021). Developing intersectional evidence can enable social policy to reflect the heterogeneity of higher education systems and communities (see, for example, Garcia and Zajicek, 2022). Social policy can aid in advancing intersectional approaches in HE through such measures as mandating attention to overlapping inequalities (Beeckmans et al., 2025; Van Laer et al., 2025), with the UK's Equality Act 2010 (covering nine 'protected characteristics') as one example where a stronger intersectional approach should be applied. It is through an intersectional lens on social policy that we can ask disruptive questions including:

- What problem is this policy intended to address?
- Who identified it as a problem, and why?
- Who is benefiting from the current situation?
- Who is being disadvantaged?
- What interventions would improve outcomes for the intersectionally disadvantaged?

We encourage you to ask these questions to policy makers to better understand their impact in HE.

Intersectional sector policy

Higher education sector-level policies are often pitted between changes in international policy, social policy, and institutional policies. It is in this space where higher education policies across the sector offer opportunities to form a collective voice. Such policies are often convened by national representative bodies, policy think tanks, and centres of insight (see, for example, IMANI Africa, n.d..; CGHE (n.d.); HEPI, n.d.; IHEP, n.d.; CGHE, n.d.; UNESCO International Institute for Higher Education in Latin America and the Caribbean, 2023; IHEP, n.d.; Steinhardt Institute for Higher Education Policy, 2025; Universities UK, 2019; de Wit and Altbach, 2020). Representative bodies and centres of excellence for higher education exist across the world to help convene conversations among and on behalf of higher education institutions. These operate to contribute, inform, influence, and challenge social and sector policy development and implementation (see, for example, Orphan et al., 2021; Jessani et al., 2022; Camp, 2021; Paulissen et al., 2022).

It is important to note here that higher education systems are uniquely positioned to both contribute evidence that can tackle oppressive social policies, while innovating and taking action to develop sector policies to challenge intersectional inequalities (see Lincoln and Stanley, 2021; Ennser-Kananen and Saarinen, 2022). It is in this space where higher education providers can collaborate and work together to inform changes. An intersectional sector policy is one that can engage community voices from diverse groups while directly challenging social policies that harm disadvantaged and underrepresented communities. For example, in the UK there is wide recognition of the role of awarding gaps between Black and white student groups across higher education, which we know impacts graduate outcomes (Banerjee, 2024; Boero et al., 2024; Mirza and Warwick, 2024). Higher education representative bodies and think tanks have collectively responded through interconnected policies that aim to proactively address the gaps at a sector level, for example, widening access and student success plans (see Universities UK, 2022; Castle, 2024). These sector-wide knowledge contributions have gone on to inform institutional policy development and implementation plans to directly tackle inequalities in higher education student experiences and outcomes (Mellors and Vicencio, 2025; Mawdsley et al., 2024; Cagliesi et al., 2024).

Arun (one of the authors of this chapter) has seen first-hand the power of higher education providers working together in having a united voice in response to political challenges. During the time he was in charge of the UK's Race Equality Charter,[1] (Advance HE, 2024) the organisation received a letter from a then senior and influential political figure, which spread misinformation that such a race equality framework undermined free speech in HE (Grove, 2022; Turner, 2022). The heavy-handed nature of the misinformed claim was rapidly refuted when Arun co-led and facilitated higher education providers, leaders, and influencers coming together to share a united message to the sector and wider society (Advance HE, 2021; Adams, 2022). The sector's response was positively received and led to Arun being invited to deliver evidence to the Women and Equalities Committee (2022). It was here, Arun brought to light the importance of high-quality evidence to inform sector policy change and influence. In this example, as a result of joining up on a position and showcasing why tackling racism matters, there was an evidenced increase in universities adopting the Race Equality Charter to help eradicate racism and intersectional inequalities in their institutions (Advance HE, 2021.; Nwosu, 2024). This case highlights the value of sector-wide policies and empowering collective voices to both challenge oppressive social policy positions and empower actions to improve outcomes for intersectionally disadvantaged and underrepresented communities (Bianchi et al., 2021).

Indeed, sector policies can advance intersectional policy making in HE through such measures as including equality-related eligibility criteria for research funding and providing certifications, such as in the case of the Race Equality Charter does (Van Laer et al., 2025).

When reflecting on intersectional sector policies, we need to think about:

- How might collective positioning on issues of intersectional injustice be used to strengthen commitment, investment, and discussion on why tackling inequality matters?
- In what ways can university partnerships take a multi-agency approach to strengthen understanding and embed intersectionality to tackle issues facing the higher education sector?
- How are leaders and influencers actively listening to those experiencing intersectional injustice to inform diligent and thoughtful approaches to tackling inequalities that are rife across the sector?

Intersectional institutional policies

Institutional level policy is informed by international, national, regional, and local social policy and sector policy. It is the realm of institutional policies that can bring to the surface how policies should respond and be put into practice. Throughout our careers we have connected with a variety of senior leaders, student leaders, and stakeholders who have at various times reacted and responded too quickly. This has meant being caught in a risk-averse state of decision paralysis or submitting to oppressive social policy. These dynamics can be seen clearly in the contemporary United States (US), where institutions have responded very differently to executive-level pressure to rescind diversity, equity, and inclusion (DEI) initiatives. It is often the case that those who are most underrepresented and marginalised will be most adversely impacted by the decisions that institutions make. However, we argue that institutions are intersectional by nature (Hawkseworth, 2003; Brown, 2014; Christoffersen and Siow, 2024). It is not just the best practice but the right practice for institutions to engage their communities who experience intersectional inequities in developing, implementing, and evaluating policies. This engagement should shape and positively disrupt oppressive power structures in higher education institutions while developing sophisticated approaches to social policy challenges (Harpur et al., 2022; Fay et al., 2020; Thomas et al., 2021). As Lukkien et al. (2024) argue, 'scholars and practitioners [in HE] should be conscious of intersectionality at every stage of policymaking: in analysing and researching the cause of inequalities, designing new and implementing more inclusive policies and practices, and perhaps most importantly, evaluating the efficacy of those practices' (p.727).

To date, the literature on intersectionality and equity policy in the field of higher education and research is limited, though this is a growing area of discussion (Beeckmans et al., 2025, 2023; Jaquetto Pereira, 2025). Existing studies provide evidence of experience of intersecting inequities for minoritised staff and students and make recommendations for policy change. Scholars have noted that ambiguity around what intersectionality means and how it should be applied has led to discrepancies between policy makers and researchers, which hamper the design and implementation of intersectional policies (Christoffersen, 2024). Moreover, intersectionality is frequently depoliticised in (neoliberal) policy discussions and often emptied of attention to race, especially in Europe (Jaquetto Pereira, 2025). Indeed, the majority of available studies discussing intersectionality and staff in HE are focused upon gender, and similarly, while some institutional policies purport to be intersectional, they remain focused upon gender (Beeckmans et al., 2023; Ruggi and Duvvury, 2022; Harpur et al., 2022). Moreover, there is a lack of research in this area concerning the Global South (Beeckmans et al., 2025, 2023). Other research in the Canadian context focuses on racialisation and Indigeneity (Henry et al., 2017), including how universities are sites of racialisation and critically scrutinising equity policies for failing to impact the experiences of racialised and Indigenous staff.

A review conducted as part of the Horizon Europe INSPIRE (CORDIS, 2024) project found that, while there is evidence of increased (nominal) commitment to diversity and inclusion at institutional level, there is a wide absence of intersectional approaches (Beeckmans et al., 2023), and this is often reduced to merely listing categories (Jaquetto Pereira 2025). This serves to overlook the experiences of women of colour (Bourabain and Verhaeghe, 2022), and indeed to silence them (Lipinsky et al., 2025), including those in not only academic but also professional roles (Muchecheti, 2025). Moreover, some categories of inequity (for example, class, sexual orientation, disability) are frequently omitted from discussion in the related literature (Beeckmans et al., 2023). Institutions need to be held accountable for developing and implementing robust policies aiming to reduce intersecting inequities. These are approaches that would be expected to create systems level change and improve representation (for example, positive action), which are notably absent in much guidance concerning HE and intersectionality. In the existing literature, evidence-based policy recommendations that have been put forward to advance intersectionality in HE include the following (Beeckmans et al., 2023; Lukkien et al., 2024; Palmén and INSPIRE Consortium, 2025):

- Participation (and remuneration) of those most intersectionality disadvantaged in policy development, implementation, and evaluation.
- Data collection on intersecting inequities.
- Community building for marginalised and intersectionally marginalised communities within universities (for example, affinity groups for staff and students).
- Hiring and promoting intersectionally marginalised staff (utilising positive or affirmative action, where legally applicable) and improving procedures concerning recruitment and promotion in a variety of ways (Lukkien et al. 2024). It is important to develop and implement such policies with the participation of intersectionally marginalised staff and to do so in ways that avoid tokenism.
- Positive action measures for minoritised students (for example dedicated scholarships).

- Measures to improve work-life balance, particularly for marginalised academics.
- Measures to raise awareness and competence in diversity (for example, training). However, the efficacy of some of these interventions for creating structural and system change has been questioned (Dobbin and Kalev, 2018).
- Increasing personal accountability for acts of discrimination, sufficiently resourcing measures for prevention and intervention.
- Improved recognition of and remuneration for equity service work (for instance, by incorporation of this service into workload models and promotion criteria).
- Provision of various types of support for intersectionally marginalised staff and students (Lukkien et al. 2024).

Research has also shed light on the enabling and hindering factors to developing intersectional policies within institutions (Van Laer et al., 2025). Facilitating factors include:

- expertise and familiarity with the concept of intersectionality
- support of senior leadership for intersectional policy making
- organisational structures supporting intersectional policy making (horizontal and vertical)
- increased internal diversity

Hindering factors include:

- lack of resources for intersectional policy making
- lack of ownership of and accountability for the implementation of intersectional policies
- persisting dominance of gender in (intersectional) equality policy making
- lack of intersectional data
- vertical or horizontal segregation of (intersectionally) minoritised groups

While these recommendations have been made, it is also stressed that there is no 'one size fits all' solution, and the different contexts of particular institutions are important to consider (Lukkien et al., 2024) in line with intersectionality theory. There are, overall, a lack of specific recommendations in the literature that address systems and structural change within institutions (Lukkien et al., 2024).

When reflecting on intersectionality in institutional policies, the wording and acknowledgement of 'intersectionality' is often only contained within equality and inclusion objectives and strategies. However, it is interesting that universities appear to not embrace the reality that they serve intersectional communities. These are communities of people who are students and staff, and a majority of these may be experiencing various forms of intersecting injustice. If we are speaking to the roots of intersectionality, we should also pay particular attention to how our institutional policies address intersecting gender, race, and class injustices that impact people, particularly Black and minority ethnic women, in higher education systems.

Arun has often been asked what an intersectional institutional policy looks like in action. The suggestion he always gives when he is delivering talks is to look at the example of counselling and welfare services that any university in the world may provide. Let's say that an institution's wellbeing policy commits to training all the staff and counsellors to develop cultural humility and understand intersectional inequality. This might involve training counsellors to support students who experience intersecting sexist, racist, and ableist oppression. Not only does the counselling service support students, many of whom may never have thought they would be welcome, heard, or seen in this environment, but the counsellors will be able to better serve the whole student community and embrace a holistic and anticipatory framework for wellbeing (see, for example, Timothy and Garcia, 2020; Adames et al., 2018).

The counselling services of most universities can often be quite small, or in some institutions they are outsourced to external organisations. The key principle here is that by designing an institutional policy, strategy, or direction of travel with intersectionality at the start, we are able to show, evidence, and demonstrate that in our university sector, no one is left behind because of who they are.

Bridging higher education policy and practice

Practitioners in HE may variously, design, implement, or evaluate institution-level policy. They do so within the constraints of international, governmental, and sectoral level policy. Dedicated equality, diversity, and inclusion (EDI) practitioners and leaders are often from racially minoritised backgrounds; isolated in their institutions; lacking institutional seniority, support, or resources; and facing resistance from colleagues (Christoffersen et al., 2023). They work with a range of others in attempting to mitigate intersectional inequities in HE. As discussed earlier in the chapter, sector-level policy may provide a positive source of support and influence within institutions.

Policy is often written at a high level, necessitating guidance for its implementation. Higher education institutions are complex, and this implementation covers various functions:

- workplace inclusion for staff (Carlow College, 2022)
- teaching and learning (Kapilashrami, 2021)
- the work of cross-institutional equality and diversity practitioners in HE (Equality Challenge Unit, 2018)
- student activism (NUS, 2014)
- those supporting students in both HE and FE (SPARQS et al., 2018)

Such guidance is important because policy does not always translate into effective action (Idahosa, 2020; Täuber, 2022). Even intersectionally informed policies in design are not always consistently translated into practice (Van Laer et al., 2025).

In recent years, policy-relevant guidance on applying intersectionality in a range of fields has proliferated (Christoffersen et al., 2025; for a full inventory of guidance, see IIRP, 2025). As part of this trend, particular guidance on using intersectionality in higher education has emerged, including in the UK:[2] 'NUS Women's Campaign's Intersectionality 101—For campuses and organizing' (NUS, 2014); 'Intersectional Approaches to Equality and Diversity in Higher Education' (Equality Challenge Unit 2018); 'Intersectionality Checklist' (SPARQS et al., 2018) in Scotland; 'Intersectionality-informed Framework for Tackling Racism and Embedding Inclusion and Diversity in Teaching and Learning' (Kapilashrami, 2021); and 'Intersectionality Guide' (Carlow College, 2022) in Ireland.

This guidance has different intended uses, with some focusing upon staff workplace inclusion (Carlow College, 2022), teaching and learning (Kapilashrami, 2021), the work of cross-institutional equality and diversity practitioners in HE (Equality Challenge Unit, 2018), and finally student activism (NUS, 2014) and those supporting students in both HE and Further Education (FE) (SPARQS et al., 2018).

However, along with guidance targeting other sectors (Christoffersen et al., 2025), some of these resources have shortfalls. For example, first, some of this guidance prioritises particular populations, namely women, thereby positioning gender as the entry point or the most important inequality, with other inequalities being 'added on' to a gender approach. This results in some additive definitions of intersectionality, for example: 'A framework for understanding how people with multiple marginalised identities (particularly women of colour) experience discrimination as a result of imbalanced power relationships in society' (Carlow College, 2022, n.p.).

Here, the use of the word 'multiple' connotes an additive approach, where identities can be added and subtracted from one another, rather than having different complex aspects shaping and ultimately becoming indivisible from one another. This is also an individualised definition of intersectionality, focusing upon identity and experience rather than systems, structures, and institutions or power relations. Power relations are identified as 'imbalanced' rather than causing significant harm to some while privileging (granting unearned advantages to) others. This guidance also predominantly identifies individualised solutions, such as increasing awareness, recognising one's own biases, and changing behaviours, rather than essential structural or system-level change. Indeed, this focus on the 'empowerment' of those experiencing intersecting inequalities, in a deficit model where the 'problem' is often located as being within minoritised communities rather than institutions, is echoed in the wider literature on intersectionality and HE (for a review, see Beeckmans et al., 2025, 2023; Jaquetto Pereira, 2025). Conversely, other guidance provides accurate, mutually constitutive definitions of intersectionality:

> In higher education, for example, students cannot be defined solely based on their skin colour or nationality. Their experience of discrimination is unique, resulting from the complex interaction of different aspects of their social location (gender, class, ethnicity, sexuality, disability). A transformative approach to education thus demands recognition of the diverse realities and embodied experiences of their socio-political, economic, and cultural lives.
>
> (Kapilashrami, 2021, para. 2)

Second, new guidance does not necessarily position itself with or build upon existing guidance (such as, for example, the Intersectionality-Based Policy Analysis framework; see Hankivsky et al., 2014); and third, there is at times little focus on structural or political factors that shape intersecting inequalities. Relatedly, fourth, while guidance identifies the vulnerability of people experiencing inequities, it does not always identify or centre agency of these groups; as such, it does not always call for the participation of communities experiencing intersecting inequities in guidance implementation. Finally, guidance often does not discuss the positionality or knowledges of the authors or identify reflexive practice as important to intersectional practice.

The guidance identifies enabling factors for intersectional practice in HE, including 'a commitment to such critical reflection, dialogue, and change' (Kapilashrami, 2021), as well as barriers including specific challenges in particular disciplines.

Overall, there is a need for more examples, case studies, and evaluation of existing policy-relevant guidance about intersectionality, as well as for more guidance that avoids the pitfalls mentioned earlier in the chapter (Christoffersen et al., 2025).

What could an intersectionality policy framework look like in HE?

There are many facets to designing, developing, and implementing intersectional policies. However, there is a need to consider what a higher education policy framework could look like to help organisations design policies with intersectionality from the outset. When deciding what an intersectionality policy framework should comprise of, it can be useful to reflect on the tenets of intersectionality, which indicate that a policy should be designed and implemented by:

- Centring the voices and participation of communities who are most intersectionally marginalised in a system and society.
- Promoting the use of storytelling to connect people's experiences to the inadequacy of policies that continue to create silos.
- Developing a 'challenge panel' of people who are intersectionally disadvantaged to encourage a variety of views that challenge group think.
- Identifying opportunities to transfer and scale the policy insights and positions that benefit a wider society that dismantles polarisation and focuses on joyful unity.
- Acknowledging and valuing that while everyone is positioned within intersecting structures of inequity, there are particular groups who are not seen, not heard, and are disempowered when it comes to participating in the decisions that impact them the most.

Reflective questions

- As a policy contributor and/or maker, what can you do to integrate intersectionality into your policy making processes and evaluation practices?
- Who is not seen or heard in your policies, and can you engage and enable their participation so they can be part of the changes that impact them the most? Who is overrepresented and has unearned advantages?
- What more can you do to support a broader intersectional frame that tackles policy silos and narrow clauses that divide rather than unite communities?
- What will you do to share practices and learnings that would enable you to generate communities that could collectively develop more awareness and engagement regarding intersectionality in policy?

Notes

1 The Race Equality Charter is a peer-reviewed framework facilitated by Advance HE that universities subscribe to. It is for UK institutions to work towards advancing race equality and tackling racism. https://www.whenequality.org/

2 These forms of guidance were identified as part of a scoping review of policy-relevant intersectionality guidance (Christoffersen et al., 2025).

References

Adams, R. (2022). Universities to defy government pressure to ditch race equality group. *The Guardian*. 30 June. Available at: https://www.theguardian.com/education/2022/jun/30/universities-to-defy-government-pressure-to-ditch-race-equality-group [Accessed 18 May 2025].

Adames, H.Y., Chavez-Dueñas, N.Y., Sharma, S., and La Roche, M.J. (2018). Intersectionality in psychotherapy: The experiences of an AfroLatinx queer immigrant. *Psychotherapy*, 55(1), pp.73–79. https://doi.org/10.1037/pst0000152.

Advance HE (2021). The relevance of the Race Equality Charter. Advance HE. Available at: https://www.advance-he.ac.uk/news-and-views/relevance-race-equality-charter [Accessed 18 May 2025].

Advance HE (2024). The Updated Race Equality Charter. Advance HE. Available at: http://advance-he.ac.uk/equality-charters/race-equality-charter [Accessed 29 Jul. 2025].

Altbach, P. G., & Knight, J. (2007). The Internationalization of Higher Education: Motivations and Realities. *Journal of Studies in International Education*, *11*(3–4), 290–305. https://doi.org/10.1177/1028315307303542.

Bagilhole, B. (2010). Applying the lens of intersectionality to UK equal opportunities and diversity policies. *Canadian Journal of Administrative Sciences/Revue Canadienne des Sciences de l'Administration*, 27(3), pp.263–271.

Banerjee, P. (2024). Connecting the dots: A systematic review of explanatory factors linking contextual indicators, institutional culture and degree awarding gaps. *Higher Education Evaluation and Development*, 18(1), pp.31–52. https://doi.org/10.1108/heed-07-2023-0020.

Beeckmans, J., Zanoni, P., and Van Laer, K. (2023). D2.1d Intersectional policies in Higher Education and Research: a scoping literature review. *Zenodo*. https://doi.org/10.5281/zenodo.10033571.

Beeckmans, J. Y. M., Zanoni, P., and Van Laer, K. (2025). Intersectionality and equality policies in higher education and research organizations: A critical scoping review and future research agenda. *Higher Education Research & Development*, pp.1–18. https://doi.org/10.1080/07294360.2025.2573980.

Bianchi, C., Nasi, G., and Rivenbark, W.C. (2021). Implementing collaborative governance: Models, experiences, and challenges. *Public Management Review*, 23(11), pp.1–9. https://doi.org/10.1080/14719037.2021.1878777.

Boero, G., Karanja, B., Naylor, R., and Thiele, T. (2024). Awarding gaps in higher education by ethnicity, schooling and family background: A UK university case study. *Education Economics*, 33(3), pp.1–16. https://doi.org/10.1080/09645292.2024.2357652.

Bourabain, D. and P.-P. Verhaeghe. (2022). Shiny on the outside, rotten on the inside? Perceptions of female early career researchers on diversity policies in higher education institutions. *Higher Education Policy*, 35(2), pp.542–60. https://doi.org/10.1057/s41307-021-00226-0.

Brown, N. (2014). *Sisters in the statehouse*. New York: Oxford University Press.

Browne, K.E., Dzebo, A., Iacobuţă, G., Faus Onbargi, A., Shawoo, Z., Dombrowsky, I., et al. (2023). How does policy coherence shape effectiveness and inequality? Implications for sustainable development and the 2030 Agenda. *Sustainable Development*, 31(5), pp.3161–3174. https://doi.org/10.1002/sd.2598.

Cagliesi, G., Hawkes, D., and Smith, S. (2024). Narrowing awarding gaps: The contributory role of institutional policy and assessment type. *Studies in Higher Education*, 48(11). https://doi.org/10.1080/03075079.2023.2209597.

Camp, M.J. (2021). No longer exempt: Higher education's entrée into lobbying. Available at: https://www.proquest.com/openview/593b7fcc9d375ff9584590a81646b481/1 [Accessed 18 May 2025].

Carlow College, St. Patrick's and the Institute of Technology Carlow (2022). Intersectionality guide. Available at: https://iadt.ie/wp-content/uploads/2022/04/Intersectionality-Guide.pdf [Accessed 6 April 2026].

Castle, K. (2024). Mapping awarding gaps. HEPI. Available at: https://www.hepi.ac.uk/2024/05/08/mapping-awarding-gaps/ [Accessed 18 May 2025].

CGHE (n.d.). Centre for Global Higher Education | An ESRC & OFSRE investment. CGHE. Available at: https://www.researchcghe.org/ [Accessed 18 May 2025].

Chankseliani, M., Qoraboyev, I., and Gimranova, D. (2020). Higher education contributing to local, national, and global development: New empirical and conceptual insights. *Higher Education*, 81(1), pp.109–127. https://doi.org/10.1007/s10734-020-00565-8.

Christoffersen, A. (2024). *The politics of intersectional practice: Representation, coalition and solidarity in UK NGOs.* Bristol: Bristol University Press.

Christoffersen, A. and Siow, O. (2024). There is no such thing as "women's representation": Intersectionality and second-generation gender and politics scholarship. *European Journal of Politics and Gender*, 8(3), 670–691.

Christoffersen, A., Hunting G., and Hankivsky, O. (2025). Integrating intersectionality in policy: A review and analysis of guidance. *Canadian Public Policy*, 51(3), pp.363–383.

Christoffersen, A., Lai, A., and Meer, N. (2023). Introduction: Racial justice work in higher education in 2023. In A. Christoffersen, A. Lai, and N. Meer, eds. *Advancing racial equality in higher education.* Edinburgh: RACE.ED and *Identities: Global Studies in Culture and Power.*

CORDIS (2024). *Intersectional spaces of participation: Inclusive, resilient, embedded.* CORDIS European Commission. Available at: https://cordis.europa.eu/project/id/101132292 [Accessed 24 July 2025].

Courtois, A. (2018). Study abroad as governmentality: The construction of hypermobile subjectivities in higher education. *Journal of Education Policy*, 35(2), pp.237–257. https://doi.org/10.1080/02680939.2018.1543809.

de Wit, H. and Altbach, P.G. (2020). Internationalization in higher education: Global trends and recommendations for its future. *Policy Reviews in Higher Education*, 5(1), pp.28–46. https://doi.org/10.1080/23322969.2020.1820898.

Deuel, R.P. (2021). Governing higher education toward neoliberal governmentality: A Foucauldian discourse analysis of global policy agendas. *Globalisation, Societies and Education*, 20(3), pp.1–14. https://doi.org/10.1080/14767724.2021.1897000.

Dobbin, F. and Alexandra Kalev. (2018). Why doesn't diversity training work? The challenge for industry and academia. *Anthropology Now*, 10(2), 48–55. https://doi.org/10.1080/19428200.2018.1493182.

Douglas Oloyede, F., Christoffersen, A., and Cornish, T. (2021). *Race Equality Charter Review*. London: Advance HE.

Eigenmann, L., Guschke, B. L., and Zippel, K. (2024). Intersectional transformation or 'gender equality+'? Intersectionality in European Union policies on research and science. *European Journal of Politics and Gender*. https://doi.org/10.1332/25151088Y2024D000000053.

Ennser-Kananen, J. and Saarinen, T. (2022). Can you imagine? An imaginary of Finland's higher education as anti-oppressive, intersectional practice. In M. Sommier, A. Roiha, and M. Lahti, eds. *Interculturality in higher education: Putting critical approaches into practice*. London: Routledge, pp.11–26.

Equality Challenge Unit. (2018). Intersectional approaches to equality and diversity in higher education. Available at: https://www.advance-he.ac.uk/knowledge-hub/intersectional-approaches-equality-and-diversity

Fay, D.L., Hicklin Fryar, A., Meier, K.J. and Wilkins, V. (2020). Intersectionality and equity: Dynamic bureaucratic representation in higher education. *Public Administration*, 99(2). https://doi.org/10.1111/padm.12691.

Garcia, T.C. and Zajicek, A. (2022). Incorporating intersectionality in public policy: A systematic literature review. *Humanity & Society*, 46(2), p.016059762098859. https://doi.org/10.1177/0160597620988591.

Grove, J. (2022). Donelan tells universities to consider leaving equality schemes. *Times Higher Education (THE)*. Available at: https://www.timeshighereducation.com/news/donelan-tells-universities-consider-leaving-equality-schemes [Accessed 18 May 2025].

Hankivsky, O., Grace, D., Hunting, G., Giesbrecht, M., Fridkin, A., Rudrum, A., et al. (2014). An intersectionality-based policy analysis framework: Critical reflections on a methodology for advancing equity. *International Journal for Equity in Health*, 13(119). https://doi.org/10.1186/s12939-014-0119-x.

Harpur, P., Szucs, B. and Willox, D. (2022). Strategic and policy responses to intersectionality in higher education. *Journal of Higher Education Policy and Management*, 45(1), pp.1–17. https://doi.org/10.1080/1360080x.2022.2144790.

Hawkesworth, M. (2003). Congressional enactments of race–gender: Toward a theory of raced–gendered institutions. *American Political Science Review*, 97(4), pp.529–50.

Henry, F., Dua, E., James, C.E., Kobayashi, A., Li, P., Ramos, H, and Smith, M.S. 2017. *The equity myth: Racialization and Indigeneity at Canadian universities*. Vancouver: UBC Press.

HEPI (n.d.). HEPI: Higher Education Policy Institute. Available at: https://www.hepi.ac.uk/.

IHEP (n.d.). IHEP: Institute for Higher Education Policy. Available at: https://www.ihep.org/ [Accessed 18 May 2025].

Idahosa GE. (2020) Dirty Body Politics: Habitus, Gendered Embodiment, and the Resistance to Women's Agency in Transforming South African Higher Education. *Gender Work Organ.* 2020(27), pp.988–1003. https://doi.org/10.1111/gwao.12425

IMANI Africa (n.d.). IMANI Centre for Policy and Education. Available at: https://imaniafrica.org/ [Accessed 18 May 2025].

Institute for Intersectionality Research and Policy (IIRP) (2025). Intersectionality guidance: An inventory. Vancouver: Institute for Intersectionality Research and Policy. Available at: www.intersectionalityinstitute.ca

Jaquetto Pereira, B.C. (2025). Reimagining equality in EU higher education and research policies: Insights from Black feminism. *Journal of Gender Studies*, 1–18. https://doi.org/10.1080/09589236.2025.2573479.

Jessani, N.S., Ling, B., Babcock, C., Valmeekanathan, A., and Holtgrave, D.R. (2022). Advocacy, activism, and lobbying: How variations in interpretation affects ability for academia to engage with public policy. PLOS Global Public Health, 2(3), p.e0000034. https://doi.org/10.1371/journal.pgph.0000034.

Jones, E., Leask, B., Brandenburg, U., and de Wit, H. (2021). Global social responsibility and the internationalisation of higher education for society. *Journal of Studies in International Education*, 25(4), pp.330–347. https://doi.org/10.1177/10283153211031679.

Kaiser, F., Maassen, P., Meek, L., van Vught, F., de Weert, E., and Goedegebuure, L., eds. (2014). *Higher education policy: An international comparative perspective.* Oxford: Pergamom Press.

Kapilashrami, A. (2021). *Intersectionality-informed framework for tackling racism and embedding inclusion and diversity in teaching and learning.* School of Health & Social Care, University of Essex. Available at: https://s3.eu-west-2.amazonaws.com/assets.creode.advancehe-document-manager/documents/advance-he/2021%2004%2012%20Intersectional%20EDI%20framework%20for%20HE_1618994584.pdf [Accessed 6 April 2026].

Klein, B., Generous, N., Chinazzi, M., Bhadricha, Z., Gunashekar, R., Kori, P., et al. (2022). Higher education responses to COVID-19 in the United States: Evidence for the impacts of university policy. PLOS Digital Health, 1(6), p.e0000065. https://doi.org/10.1371/journal.pdig.0000065.

Lincoln, Y.S. and Stanley, C.A. (2021). The faces of institutionalized discrimination and systemic oppression in higher education: Uncovering the lived experience of bias and procedural inequity. *Qualitative Inquiry*, 27(10), p.107780042110268. https://doi.org/10.1177/10778004211026892.

Lipinsky, A., Jaquetto Pereira, B., and Pilinkaitė Sotirovič, V. (2025). Embracing paradox realities: Racially minoritised women and gender-based violence in higher education. *Social Inclusion, 14*, Article 9825.

Lukkien, T., Chauhan, T., and Otaye-Ebede, L. (2024). Addressing the diversity principle–practice gap in Western higher education institutions: A systematic review on intersectionality. *British Educational Research Journal*, 51(2), 705–736. https://doi.org/10.1002/berj.4096.

Marginson, S. (2011). Higher education and public good. *Higher Education Quarterly*, 65(4), pp.411–433. https://doi.org/10.1111/j.1468-2273.2011.00496.x.

Mawdsley, A., Magola-Makina, E., and Willis, S.C. (2024). Towards addressing the awarding gap—Using critical race theory to contextualise the role of intersectionality in Black pharmacy student attainment. *Medical Education*, 58(10), pp.1235–1246. https://doi.org/10.1111/medu.15460.

Mellors, J. and Vicencio, A. (2025). Widening participation in outward student mobility: Successes, challenges, and opportunities. *British Educational Research Journal*, 51(5), pp.2358–2376. https://doi.org/10.1002/berj.4176.

Mirza, H.S. and Warwick, R. (2024). Race and ethnic inequalities. *Oxford Open Economics*, 3(1), pp.i365–i452. https://doi.org/10.1093/ooec/odad026.

Molla, T. (2020). Refugees and equity policy in Australian higher education. *Policy Reviews in Higher Education*, 5(1), pp.1–23. https://doi.org/10.1080/23322969.2020.1806727.

Muchecheti, A. (2025). *The lived experiences of a non-academic woman of colour working in uk higher education*. New York: Lived Places Publishing.

Murtaza, K.G. and Hui, L. (2021). Higher education in Pakistan: Challenges, opportunities, suggestions. *Education Quarterly Reviews*, 4(2), pp.213–219. https://doi.org/10.31014/aior.1993.04.02.211.

NUS (National Union of Students) (2014). Intersectionality 101—For campuses and organizing. Available at: https://www.nusconnect.org.uk/resources/intersectionality-101 Accessed 18 May 2025

Nwosu, C. (2024). Evaluating the impact of the race equality charter on diversity staff outcomes. *Race, Ethnicity and Education*, pp.1–11. https://doi.org/10.1080/13613324.2024.2328372.

Orphan, C.M., Laderman, S., and Gildersleeve, R.E. (2021). Advocates or honest information brokers? Examining the higher education public policy agenda-setting processes of intermediary organizations. *The Review of Higher Education*, 44(3), pp.325–355. https://doi.org/10.1353/rhe.2021.0002.

Palmén, R. and INSPIRE Consortium (2025). D3.12 European Policy Brief – Intersectionality: An in-depth focus. *Zenodo.* https://doi.org/10.5281/zenodo.15546224

Paulissen, T., Fraussen, B., and Van Hecke, S. (2022). Individual and collective representation: The organisational form of higher education lobbying in the European Union. European Journal of Higher Education, 14(1), pp.1–19. https://doi.org/10.1080/21568235.2022.2105372.

Pineda, P. and Mishra, S. (2022). The semantics of diversity in higher education: Differences between the Global North and Global South. *Higher Education*, 85(1). https://doi.org/10.1007/s10734-022-00870-4.

Platt, L. (2025). What is social policy? London School of Economics and Political Science. Available at: https://www.lse.ac.uk/social-policy/about-us/What-is-social-policy [Accessed 18 May 2025].

Qureshi, I., Gogoi, M., Al-Oraibi, A., Wobi, F., Pan, D., Martin, C.A., et al (2022). Intersectionality and developing evidence-based policy. *The Lancet*, 399(10322), pp.355–356. https://doi.org/10.1016/s0140-6736(21)02801-4.

Rizvi, F., and Lingard, B. (2010). *Globalizing Education Policy*. New York and London: Routledge.

Rodrigues, L. (2025). Beware of policies bearing gifts: How policies enable sanitized intersectionality, exclusive inclusion, and divertising. *Policy Futures in Education*, 24(2). https://doi.org/10.1177/14782103251381519

Ruggi, L.O. and Duvvury, N. (2022). Shattered glass piling at the bottom: The `problem with gender equality policy for higher education. Critical Social Policy. https://doi.org/10.1177/02610183221119717.

Salmi, J. and D'Addio, A. (2020). Policies for achieving inclusion in higher education. *Policy Reviews in Higher Education*, 5(1), pp.1–26. Available at: https://www.tandfonline.com/doi/abs/10.1080/23322969.2020.1835529 [Accessed 17 May 2025].

Schipper, E.L.F., Eriksen, S.E., Fernandez Carril, L.R., Glavovic, B.C., and Shawoo, Z. (2020). Turbulent transformation: Abrupt societal disruption and climate resilient development. *Climate and Development*, 13(6), pp.1–8. https://doi.org/10.1080/17565529.2020.1799738.

Shahjahan, R.A. (2012). The roles of international organizations (IOs) in globalizing higher education policy. In J. Smart and M.B. Paulsen, eds. *Higher education: Handbook of theory and research*. London: Springer, pp.369–407.

SPARQS (Student Partnerships in Quality Scotland), NUS Scotland Women, and Advance HE. (2018). Intersectionality checklist. Available at: https://www.sparqs.ac.uk/ch/Intersectionality%20Checklist%20FINAL%20Oct%202018.pdf[Accessed 6 April 2026].

Steinhardt Institute for Higher Education Policy (2025). Steinhardt Institute for Higher Education Policy. NYU Steinhardt. Available at: https://steinhardt.nyu.edu/sihep [Accessed 18 May 2025].

Täuber, S. (2022). Women academics' intersectional experiences of policy ineffectiveness in the European context. *Front. Psychol.* 13:810569. https://doi.org/10.3389/fpsyg.2022.810569

Thomas, C., MacMillan, C., McKinnon, M., Torabi, H., Osmond-McLeod, M., Swavley, E., et al (2021). Seeing and overcoming the complexities of intersectionality. *Challenges*, 12(1), p.5. https://doi.org/10.3390/challe12010005.

Timothy, R.K. and Umana Garcia, M. (2020). Anti-oppression psychotherapy: An emancipatory integration of intersectionality into psychotherapy. *Psychotherapy and Counselling Journal of Australia*, 8(2). https://doi.org/10.59158/001c.71085.

Turner, C. (2022). Universities told to reconsider membership of 'woke' scheme. *The Telegraph*. Available at: https://www.telegraph.co.uk/news/2022/06/27/universities-told-reconsider-membership-woke-scheme/?msockid=25a8a90d21d569f9208eba2c201368fb [Accessed 18 May 2025].

UNESCO International Institute for Higher Education in Latin America and the Caribbean (2023). HE Policy Observatory. UNESCO. Available at: https://hepo.iesalc.unesco.org/pc/page/home/ [Accessed 18 May 2025].

Universities UK (2019). Universities UK. Available at: https://www.universitiesuk.ac.uk/ [Accessed 18 May 2025].

Universities UK (2022). Closing ethnicity degree awarding gaps: three years on. [online] Universities UK. Available at: https://www.universitiesuk.ac.uk/what-we-do/policy-and-research/publications/features/closing-gap-three-years/introduction [Accessed 18 May 2025].

Van Laer, K., Zanoni, P., and Beeckmans, J. (2025). D3.5 Factors facilitating or hindering intersectional equality policy making: An explorative European multiple-case study. *Zenodo*. https://doi.org/10.5281/zenodo.15590854.

van der Wende, M. (2007). Internationalization of higher education in the OECD Countries: Challenges and opportunities for the coming decade. *Journal of Studies in International Education*, 11(3–4), pp.274–289. https://doi.org/10.1177/1028315307303543.

Ward, S.C., Bagley, C., Lumby, J., Hamilton, T., Woods, P., and Roberts, A. (2015). What is 'policy' and what is 'policy response'? An illustrative study of the implementation of the Leadership Standards for Social Justice in Scotland. *Educational Management Administration & Leadership*, 44(1), pp.43–56. https://doi.org/10.1177/1741143214558580.

Williams, F. (2021). *Social policy: A critical and intersectional analysis*. Cambridge: Polity Press.

Wilson, C. L., Singh, A. K., Beals, A. M., Sharma, R., Hunt, B., Furman, E., et al. (2021). Dialogues of disruption: Confronting oppression in the academy. Global Journal of Community Psychology Practice, 12(3). https://doi.org/10.17161/gjcpp.v12i3.20638.

Women and Equalities Committee (2022). Racial harassment and discrimination in higher education (one-off session). London: UK Parliament. Available at: https://committees.parliament.uk/event/13492/formal-meeting-oral-evidence-session/ [Accessed 18 May 2025].

Yonezawa, A. (2023). Japan's higher education policies under global challenges. *Asian Economic Policy Review*, 18(2). https://doi.org/10.1111/aepr.12421.

4

An intersectional approach to data

Kevin Guyan

In UK higher education, it can seem like everyone is talking about data. Plans to 'address data gaps' (Gustave, 2023), collect 'more robust data' (Corner, 2025), and 'empower staff by giving them access to the data they need' (Universities UK, 2022) are promoted as the way forward. In discussions about diversity data, where data is collected about staff and students' identity characteristics, references are made to an 'intersectional' approach (Cardiff University, 2024; Congdon, 2021; Millward, 2020). But what *actually* is an 'intersectional approach' to data? And does it offer anything different from non-intersectional approaches?

This chapter presents an account of how intersectionality is applied to quantitative data practices in higher education, examining what an intersectional approach to data entails and the challenges that arise when this approach is adopted. Quantitative data practices cover a broad sweep of activities, including the collection and analysis of results from diversity monitoring exercises (for example, totals, averages, statistical significance), benchmarking of data against comparator institutions (for example, league tables), collation of data for accreditation schemes (for example, Advance HE's Athena SWAN and Race Equality Charters), and publishing of data as tables, graphs, and other visualisations. At its most elemental, an intersectional approach asks questions about the individual data subject: who are they? Where do the borders of the data subject start and end? Who is included and excluded from consideration? And how does one data subject interact with another? In higher education, a data subject is usually an individual student or staff member, with information collected about who they are (including gender, age, race, sexual orientation) and what they do (including job role, degree enrolment) as they move through the institution.

An intersectional approach to data highlights what is lost or obscured when a single strand of a person's identity (for example, their gender or race) is the sole focus of enquiry. It involves more than adding extra columns to an Excel spreadsheet or running cross-tabulated analysis. An intersectional approach is embedded from the inception of a data project rather than retrofitted after all design decisions are already confirmed. In this chapter, I intentionally use the term 'intersectional approach' to highlight that I am not describing a 'type' of data (for example, quantitative data or ordinal data) but a mindset, mood, or way of thinking. An intersectional approach to data should make you feel something and inspire you to work differently. It is a type of practice, not a type of knowledge.

As an action-oriented approach, understanding gender, race, and class as intersecting creates a politics that requires data practitioners to look beyond 'the numbers' and more fully examine the network of power relations that spark against data as it moves through collection, analysis, and use. In higher education, and other institutional contexts, there is often an assumption that identities exist as sortable and stable categories (Clair et al., 2019), and that people will disclose information about who they are because they believe this sharing of information will make the institution better. Yet, the identity categories plugged into counting machines are neither natural nor universal, and only make sense in the contexts where they are deployed (Bowker and Star, 1999). In this sense, numbers are always political – even when deliberations over who to count and how to count are obscured by a 'veil of technocracy' (Grek et al., 2023, p.2, building on the work of Porter, 1995). Yet, even though these practices determine what doors are opened and closed to us, we generally remain unaware of how classifications and sorting practices shape our experiences of the world (Bowker and Star, 1999).

In this chapter, I discuss how an intersectional approach to data is understood and operationalised in UK higher education.

In the process, I counter understandings of intersectional data as a solution (or even, *the* solution) to social inequalities in the university. I outline data developments in key sector organisations – the national statistics producer, the Office for National Statistics (ONS); the government agency responsible for quantitative information about higher education, Higher Education Statistics Agency (HESA); and the higher education charity and membership organisation, Advance HE – and note how recent efforts to change sex and gender questions have done little to advance a meaningfully intersectional approach. In addition, in three short case studies, I explore related issues in more depth. Firstly, the April 2025 UK Supreme Court decision to define 'sex' in the 2010 Equality Act as exclusively meaning 'biological sex' assigned at birth, and how judges used a critique of 'heterogenous' categories to arrive at their ruling. Secondly, assumptions embedded in metaphors used to communicate ideas about data (most notably, the idea of a leaky pipeline for staff progression). Thirdly, the issue of 'missingness' and risks associated with data harmonisation. I conclude by highlighting limitations of an intersectional approach to data, including the failure to recognise lives beyond the expected labels, the risks that accompany making categories more meaningful, and the problem of saying one thing but doing something else.

What does intersectionality mean for data?

As a gender and sexuality researcher, I spend too much time stuck in meetings deliberating definitions for certain words and concepts. Heeding my frustrations, and aware that other contributors in this collection will have already offered definitions for 'intersectionality,' I keep this section brief. Intersectionality has a long, intellectual history within Black feminism, highlighting the multitude of ways that Black women's experiences and identities were marginalised through legal, social, and political systems designed to foreground white men as the default human subject (Collins, 1990; Crenshaw, 1989, 1991). As a remedy, throughout the latter half of the 20th century, feminist and anti-racist movements succeeded in injecting gender and race analyses into the conversation. However, in many cases, this turn to diversity was premised on the idea of mutually exclusive identity categories, where social inequalities were only recognised when they sat within a single frame of discrimination (Christoffersen and Emejulu, 2023; Crenshaw, 1989). For example, a Black woman who is refused promotion because of her identity needs to choose whether to frame her discrimination claim as related to gender or race, but not both. Legal scholar Kimberlé Crenshaw's (1989, p.149) famous analogy of a traffic accident at an intersection evokes this challenge:

> Consider an analogy to traffic in an intersection, coming and going in all four directions. Discrimination, like traffic through an intersection, may flow in one direction, and it may flow in another. If an accident happens in an intersection, it can be caused by cars traveling from any number of directions and, sometimes, from all of them. Similarly, if a Black woman is harmed because she is in the intersection, her injury could result from sex discrimination or race discrimination.

The institutions that determine what problems are offered a remedy, often using data about the problem to justify this selection, demand a clear line between cause and effect. When a clear line between cause and effect is not established (or is not clear enough), then the need for a remedy is excused. Crenshaw continues (1989, p.149):

> Providing legal relief only when Black women show that their claims are based on race or on sex is analogous to calling an ambulance for the victim only after the driver responsible for the injuries is identified. But it is not always easy to reconstruct an accident: sometimes the skid marks and the injuries simply indicate that they occurred simultaneously, frustrating efforts to determine which driver caused the harm. In these cases the tendency seems to be that no driver is held responsible, no treatment is administered, and the involved parties simply get back in their cars and zoom away.

Crenshaw highlights how systems for legal recourse were designed to serve individuals marginalised due to a single issue: individuals who fit the mould of the 'default human' (in other words, a white, cisgender, straight, affluent, non-disabled man) if not for a single aspect of their identity (for example, their gender or race). However, most people's lived experiences bring together a bundle of interlocking phenomena (McCall, 2005). Siloed gender and race analyses simply do not work for everyone – a more nuanced and contextual approach is required.

Intersectionality is therefore at odds with related concepts such as 'diversity' and 'inclusion', which call for the *bringing in* of historically marginalised groups to institutions that previously kept them out. Intersectionality queries this objective and highlights the downsides of engaging more people in institutions that were intentionally built to marginalise and exclude. Gender and sexuality scholar Jennifer C. Nash (2018, p.24) notes, 'Where diversity is a project of including bodies, intersectionality is an antisubordination project, one committed to foregrounding exclusion and its effects'. When adopting an intersectional approach, it is not about adding more diverse faces; it is about root and branch reform.

An odd couple: quantitative data and intersectionality

Quantitative data practices involve observing real-world phenomena, grouping what is observed according to shared qualities (for example, all staff who are men, all students who are Chinese) so they become countable, and then arranging these items in some sort of order (for example, highest to lowest, best to worst). A tension exists between intersectionality and quantitative data practices, which are positivist and understand the world as consisting of observable phenomena that researchers can explain through the use of scientific tools (Keith, 2021). Returning to Crenshaw's analogy of a traffic accident at an intersection, her claim that 'it is not always easy to reconstruct an accident' (1989, p.149) echoes current discussions in higher education regarding the sector's continued faith in quantitative data to present problems in ways that are knowable and actionable.

As anthropologists Richard Rottenburg and Sally Engle Merry (2015, pp.7–8) note, 'Things that at first appeared incommensurable can be made commensurable. Through numeric representation, one always loses some aspects of the reality in question but gains others that were invisible before quantification'. For example, when a data scientist analyses statistics about LGBTQ students, these numbers are understood as a direct representation of the world, not an interpretation of it. Countering this view and writing on how AI represents the world, tech scholar Shannon Vallor (2024, p.133) argues, 'we are not seeing objective truths' but 'we are seeing reflections of what humans valued enough to describe or record in data'. The data systems used to determine what counts as a problem in higher education do not offer a carbon copy of the world around us. It is a representation – with some features sharpened and others dulled.

In higher education, diversity data projects (for example, reviews of academic promotions data broken down by gender and race) usually involve more than capturing single pieces of data, but instead bring together multiple items to identify patterns and problems. When data is collected in a dataset, the relationships between items are simplified and items are delinked from their wider contexts (Bentley et al., 2023, p.3). A model dataset is neat and tidy. The items contained within a dataset are discrete, each with a defined location, value, and relationship to other items (Bentley et al., 2023). Order, it is believed, produces meaning. As part of this effort to establish meaning, higher education data is routinely discussed in relation to numbers moving in a particular direction: the number of Black female professors is going up, the dropout rate among disabled students is going down. Feminist scholar Sara Ahmed (2012, p.55) describes how 'data becomes a technology for exposing the gap between official descriptions of diversity and what the organization is doing'. One of Ahmed's interviewees, a diversity worker in a UK university, described how they felt when the numbers go in the wrong direction: 'Yeah, yeah, it's embarrassing when it goes up' (Ahmed, 2012, p.55). As Ahmed's interviewee suggests, the problem of social inequalities in the university has become a problem of numbers.

What is an intersectional approach to data?

An intersectional approach to data is not necessarily a sharp break from past ways of working, which focus on a single identity strand, but an extended and more nuanced approach. An intersectional approach to data creates something more than the sum of its parts. It adds a special sauce, where A + B + C does not equal ABC but something altogether different. In fact, according to intersectionality scholar Ashlee Christoffersen (2024), we should not consider gender + race + class calculations an intersectional approach, as it suggests that identity categories can exist in isolation from other interlocking structures of inequality (Christoffersen and Emejulu, 2023, p.635; Hancock, 2019). An additive approach is therefore at odds with an intersectional approach, where the phenomenon observed is always simultaneous, multi-directional, and mutually constituting. Intersectionality, as a mindset or approach to data, does not provide a list of steps to follow (for example, A + B + C = solution). It is not a theory or something we can test. However, it is *something*. It has contours and inflexions, and – when applied in particular contexts – sharpens a selection of issues. In the following section, I provide an account of an intersectional approach to data.

Everything is interconnected

An intersectional approach to data requires data practitioners to interrogate how privilege (an advantage granted to a particular person or group) and oppression (where people are treated unjustly and have their opportunities restricted) result in multiple social inequalities at the level of the (1) individual and the (2) system (Bowleg, 2012). Now that I am a few pages into my account of intersectionality, you will not be surprised to learn that these features are not distinct but entangled. For those adopting an intersectional approach to data, analysis is therefore only possible in a data culture where social inequalities and systems of oppression are understood as 'interlocking' (Combahee River Collective, 2014, p.271). The Combahee River Collective – a group of Black, feminist, lesbian socialists active in Boston, US in the late 1970s – described how the struggle 'against racial, sexual, heterosexual, and class oppression' is collective and holistic (Combahee River

Collective, 2014, p.271). For data practitioners today, our account of the problem – and the evidence used to justify its selection – must be understood holistically. In other words, it is not possible to parse off a 'gender analysis' or a 'race analysis' because meaning derives from everything's interconnectedness.

Focus on marginalised experiences

We all possess multiple, intersecting identities. Even if your university principal is white (race), male (gender), older (age), and affluent (class), he still has an identity that consists of intersections. But not everyone is (or should be) the focus of an intersectional analysis. As social psychologist Lisa Bowleg (2012, p.1268) observes, a 'core tenet of intersectionality is its focus on the intersecting identities of people from historically oppressed and marginalized groups'. However, locating a starting point for analysis and beginning with a focus on 'marginalized groups' is easier said than done. Value judgements determine who counts as marginalised and in what contexts: being marginalised is not a status (not what someone *is*) but something that is actively done to individuals in particular times and spaces. For example, identifying as a Black, bisexual man in one part of the university can have different effects depending on the context of where it happens (Hancock, 2019). Similarly, a white, heterosexual man is not understood as privileged because of what he does (in other words, his actions) but because he is the one performing the actions (in other words, his status) (Carbado, 2013). These nuanced considerations occur against a backdrop where structural inequalities – such as institutional racism, classism, and sexism – are often apparent and easy to trace (Inclusive Data Charter, 2021, p.5). We should therefore not assume that data practitioners possess the ability to recognise the *most marginalised* in any data project (an issue I return to later in the chapter), as these experiences often tend to be 'unknown, silent, muted, unheard, and ignored' (Inclusive Data Charter, 2021, p.5).

Complexity

Ultimately, an intersectional approach to data acknowledges that navigating questions of difference involves complexity. For me, this acknowledgement of complexity is one of intersectionality's key political uses as it directly challenges ongoing calls for 'clarity' and 'coherency' in data projects about identity categories (see Sullivan, 2025). Efforts to ignore or evade complexity have dominated recent discussions in the UK about categories of sex and gender and their representation in data. Most notably, on 16 April 2025 the Supreme Court ruled that term 'sex' in the 2010 Equality Act – the key equalities legislation in England, Wales, and Scotland – means 'biological sex' assigned at birth (UK Supreme Court, 2025). A few weeks earlier, Alice Sullivan – a trans-exclusionary sociologist – published a government-commissioned review of sex and gender data in research and statistics. In the review, Sullivan called for clarity in an age where 'the meaning of sex is no longer stable in administrative or major survey data' (Sullivan, 2025, p.3).

Case Study 1: The UK Supreme Court, 'biological sex', and homogenous categories

On 16 April 2025, the UK Supreme Court ruled that the term 'sex' in the Equality Act should be interpreted as meaning 'biological sex' assigned at birth. This narrow definition of 'sex' upended a previous working understanding where 'sex' included multiple meanings related to biology, legal status, and self-identification. For data practitioners, this ruling has potential implications for how data about 'sex' is collected in higher education institutions (HEIs), particularly in contexts where data is collected for equalities reporting (for example, to demonstrate a university's activities related to the Equality Act's Public Sector Equality Duty).

In their ruling, the judges took issue with how the category of 'female' is inclusive of 'biological women, some biological males with a GRC [Gender Recognition Certificate] (trans women who are legally female) and excluding some biological females with a GRC (trans men who are legally male)'. The ruling argues that 'any data collection exercise will be distorted by the heterogenous nature of such a group'. However, arguably, the heterogenous nature of these categories reflects how they are experienced in the social world. The category of women includes a vast array of races and ethnicities, social classes, ages, and sexualities – by throwing trans women out of the category of women, the category does not become any more 'homogenous', nor should the construction of 'homogenous' categories become the objective of data practitioners.

In a turbulent present, where many aspects of the world no longer make sense, I partly understand this aversion to complexity and hunger for clear-cut meaning. An intersectional approach to data, however, does not offer simplicity. Quite the opposite: it advocates for data practices that are *more complex* (Christoffersen, 2024). But what is wrong with complexity? Life is not simple, nor is the world we wish to represent through our research tools and methods. Complex inequalities cannot be understood or addressed with simple solutions.

Ultimately, an intersectional approach promises data practitioners a better diagnosis of social inequalities and, with a better diagnosis, the potential for more effective solutions. Nash (2018, p.15) highlights, 'intersectionality's imagined goal of capturing an impossible "etc.," an account of the social universe that can attend to the unending complexity of both identity and the social world'. This promise is not unique. The use of research tools to observe, measure, and compare phenomena is common. As sociologists Wendy Nelson Espeland and Mitchell L. Stevens (2008, p.415) note, 'Quantification makes visible people, objects or characteristics that may formerly have been invisible'.

An intersectional approach to data is therefore both revelatory (in other words, it makes things visible that were once hidden) and a primer for action (in other words, it directs attention and resources to particular problems) (Bentley et al., 2023). For example, data published by Advance HE (2024) shows that in 2023–24, of the UK's 22,280 professors, just 55 were Black women (around 0.2 per cent). If understood as a problem, this revelation – a product of data collection, analysis, and presentation of what is happening in the sector – can become a target for action. As scholar Greta R. Bauer and colleagues (2021, p.224) argue, in an era of evidence-based policy making, data has 'become a lynchpin for decisions over resource allocation'.

However, when applied uncritically, these techniques risk narrowing discussions about what problems are understood as relevant and meaningful (Espeland and Stevens, 2008). Many social inequalities are not easy to quantify or translate into illustrative visualisations – should these barriers exclude them from becoming a target for action? An intersectional approach to data is therefore an extension and continuation of methods used to reveal and control complex phenomena. Noting this lineage is important because it highlights a key limitation of an intersectional approach to data: in many ways, it is not all that different from approaches that came before.

The context: higher education staff and student data

While the word 'intersectionality' is now part of the vocabulary of many data practitioners in higher education, it remains less clear whether the concept has meaningfully arrived. In this section, I situate an intersectional approach to data among the where, how, and who of data practices in the UK.

The 'where'

HEIs, funders, government agencies, and other organisations are more eager than ever to count, categorise, and measure who we are and what we do (Guyan, 2022, 2025).[1] In higher education, data about identity characteristics informs decisions made by research funders, most notably UK Research and Innovation (UKRI, 2025) and the distribution of more than £6 billion of funds across science and research. The Strategy, People and Research Environment component of the next Research Excellence Framework, scheduled to take place in 2029, also plans to review data on the diversity of researchers as part of its assessment (REF 2029, 2025). Gender equality work, in particular, has become synonymous with huge data collection and analysis projects – most notably Advance HE's Athena SWAN programme.

Many of these diversity data projects are the product of good intentions, introduced to produce insights that respond to social inequalities and create a more equitable sector. Yet, across these projects, data about one's identity characteristics sits uncomfortably alongside neoliberal approaches to diversity, equality, and inclusion work, where the data subject is individualised, stripped of its context, and plugged into counting machines. Transfeminist scholars Nat Raha and Mijke van der Drift (2024, p.37) describe neoliberalism as 'a politics of indifference that strengthens authoritarian structures, reinforcing commodified institutional logics'. Explicitly identifying a relationship between a type of intersectionality and neoliberalism, sociologist Sirma Bilge (2014) describes how a mutated appropriation of intersectionality 'has been commodified and colonized for neoliberal regimes'.

Diversity data (whether intersectional or not) provides institutions with new opportunities for measurement – a prerequisite for competition and a foundational tenet of neoliberalism. To draw comparisons and sort people into winners and losers, agreed-upon systems of measurement are required (Beer, 2016). The neoliberal arc from inclusion in data to an opening up of new frontiers for competition positions individual staff members and students as the primary target of an institution's data activities. This over-focus on the individual – as a data point to follow around an institution, through a career or learner journey – risks downplaying the effects of organisational and social contexts on a person's experiences (Zanoni et al., 2010). In previous writing (Guyan, 2025), I have described how, for LGBTQ communities, being invited into historically exclusionary institutions requires those included to align themselves with categories that do not mirror their life experiences. As political scientist Wendy Brown (2015, p.42) sharply observes, 'inclusion inverts into competition'.

The 'how'

In this section, I get more specific about the data systems where intersectionality is (or might be) operationalised. I share brief examples from key sector organisations related to sex and gender data: the ONS, HESA, and Advance HE. I focus on sex and gender data as this topic has commanded the attention of the media, politicians, and sector leaders since the late 2010s, as they sought to engage and placate an emergent anti-trans movement calling for the erasure of trans people in policy, law, and data (Amery, 2024; Collier and Cowan, 2022; Guyan, 2026). Sex and gender data are used for a variety of purposes and therefore involve asking different questions according to the proposed use of the data (Currah, 2022). For example, data about sex and gender have different purposes when used to construct a diversity profile of workers in the creative industries compared to when used in the testing of pharmaceutical products on different types of bodies. However, as I argue in this section, the higher education sector has focused too much attention on the design of sex and gender questions at the expense of exploring how systems might meaningfully embed an intersectional approach to data.

Office for National Statistics

The most high-profile data collection exercise in the UK is the national census. The Office for National Statistics (ONS), responsible for the delivery of the census in England and Wales, conducts a census every ten years with the most recent census taken on 21 March 2021. Following the addition of new questions on sexual orientation and gender identity in 2021, the census now asks questions about all nine protected characteristics in the 2010 Equality Act (sex, race, age, disability, sexual orientation, religion and belief, gender reassignment, pregnancy and maternity, and marital status). The questions asked in the census therefore tend to provide a blueprint for how data practitioners collect information about identity characteristics in specific sectors and industries.

However, this top-down approach to data invites potential risks. In March 2021, a few weeks after the English and Welsh census had gone live, the trans-exclusionary campaign group Fair Play for Women took the ONS to court to demand a change in the guidance that accompanied the census question on sex (Topping, 2021). The ONS's original guidance, based on user testing and feedback, noted: 'If you are considering how to answer, use the sex recorded on one of your legal documents such as a birth certificate, gender recognition certificate, or passport'.

Fair Play for Women's legal challenge was successful, which led to an interim ruling that forced the ONS to remove the words 'such as' and 'or passport' from the guidance so that respondents were advised to answer according to the sex recorded on their birth certificate or GRC only. The ONS chose not to defend their position, and the interim ruling was maintained, overturning years of detailed research and stakeholder consultation undertaken by the organisation. One year later, Fair Play for Women tried the same strategy with the Scottish census (BBC News, 2022), which took place in 2022. However, in this instance, National Records of Scotland (the agency responsible for Scotland's census) defended its approach and won the case. As a result, supporting guidance for the sex question differed in censuses conducted in Scotland and the rest of the UK.

Higher Education Statistical Agency

Changes have also occurred in how HESA, the agency responsible for quantitative data about staff and students in higher education, captures information about sex and gender. In 2018/19, HESA provided three response options for HEIs when reporting sex data for staff and students: 'male', 'female', and 'other' (HESA, 2018). HESA's supporting guidance notes that respondents who identify in a way other than male or female (for example, intersex, androgyne, intergender, ambigender, gender fluid, polygender, and genderqueer) may use the response option 'other'.

Case Study 2: Intersectional data and metaphors

An intersectional approach to data invites us to think critically on the metaphors we use to communicate ideas about data. A metaphor commonly used to describe an individual's career journey in higher education is that of a 'pipeline' – in particular, a 'leaky pipeline' that describes the drop-off of women reaching senior levels (Ayyildiz and Banoglu, 2024; Fabrellas, 2024). However, as researcher Jodi Watt (2023) observes, the pipeline metaphor paints a vision of the sector at odds with an intersectional approach, as a pipeline carries a gas or liquid with 'an incredibly uniform molecule', making it 'a terrible analogy for the richness and uniqueness of experience of individuals in academia'. Furthermore, the metaphor suggests a clear separation between what is inside and outside the pipeline; liquids only flow in one direction, what is being transported does not interact with the pipeline, and when a leak occurs, the pipeline needs to be fixed (Tajmel, 2019). These features of a pipeline do not reflect many people's experiences of careers in higher education and therefore highlight the need for caution with the metaphors we use when telling stories about data.

Fast forward to 2025/26 and HESA's approach to the collection of sex data had shifted in subtle ways (HESA, 2025). While response options still included 'male', 'female', and 'other' (alongside the options 'information refused' and 'not available'), HESA notes that the 'other' option should 'be used only for a third sex that is legally recognised by another country' and that this option 'will recognise the scenarios where, for example, an international staff member has a legal sex other than male or female'. HESA does not explain how a data collector, working in a university HR or DEI team, is expected to know the legal context of all countries from where staff originate and possess knowledge of the rapidly evolving landscape of 'legal sex' recognition. In addition, the 'information refused' option is not intended to meaningfully acknowledge respondents who prefer not to say, and HEIs are advised that this 'option is not presented to the data subject by default'.

Advance HE

Finally, Advance HE is a higher education organisation that manages the Athena SWAN and Race Equality Charters, publishes annual statistical reports on the diversity profile of staff and students in UK HEIs, and provides advice and guidance on equality, diversity, and inclusion issues. As recently as 2021, Advance HE (2021, p.16) recommended that HEIs ask a 'question about gender rather than asking a question about sex' as this approach 'ensures equality efforts are mindful of the different ways gendered norms and marginalisations occur, and is inclusive of a diverse range of gender identities'.[2] In their 2021 guidance, Advance HE recommended that HEIs ask the following question when collecting staff and student data:

How would you describe your gender?

+ Man
+ Non-binary
+ Woman
+ In another way (specify if you wish):
+ Prefer not to say

The guidance explained that, as this question asks about 'man' and 'woman,' data collected can be used for reporting in the small number of instances where binary data about sex is required. Advance HE (2021, p.16) also advised 'against asking about a respondent's gender **and** sex on the same monitoring form as this may confuse respondents and, when response options are combined, inadvertently out someone who identifies as trans' (bold in original).

By 2025, the picture had changed and Advance HE now advised HEIs to ask the following question about sex (2025):

What is your sex?

+ Female
+ Male
+ Prefer not to say

Advance HE (2025, p.18) justified this major change by noting that 'conflating gender identity and sex may cause confusion and could lead to challenges on the basis that the data being collected, and the decisions being taken on the back of that data do not give due regard to the specific issues which arise on grounds of sex and/or gender identity'.

I share these brief examples to highlight some developments related to sex and gender data in UK higher education since 2018. Much of this attention has prioritised the capture of data about sex and gender, rather than more expansive reviews of *all* diversity data and/or the adoption of an intersectional approach to data.

The 'who'

Finally, many hands are involved in the production of diversity data in higher education. An intersectional approach highlights a 'need to bring upfront the data labour' (Bauer, 2019, p.226) to probe the skills and competence of those responsible for doing the data work. But who are the workers responsible for making decisions about diversity data and representing lives that, in most cases, differ from their own? As previously noted, we should not assume that individuals tasked with doing data work in HEIs can recognise the *most marginalised* community or who is missing from a dataset, as these insights require a specific combination of expertise and experience. One way to mitigate these flaws is to create larger, more diverse teams so that any individual's personal omissions are, in theory, complemented by the expertise and experience of someone else (Nielsen et al., 2025).

Case Study 3: Missingness and data harmonisation

Writing on the topic of missing data, scholars Anahid Basiri and Chris Brunsdon (2022, p.1) observe how 'no comment can be a comment'. When asking people to volunteer or self-report information about themselves, we should pay attention to the multiple reasons why someone may choose to remain silent and the many factors that lead to 'missingness'. Relatedly, how a HEI responds to missingness – for example, through the capture of more data or expansion of data categories – can pose risks for individuals whose data across different systems is not consistent (Waldman, 2023). For example, a trans woman who is counted as 'male' in her HESA record but 'female' on her driving license faces potential issues when efforts are made to harmonise data collected across different administrative systems.

The limitations of an intersectional approach to data

A strength of an intersectional approach to data is its examination of differences *within* identity categories. When accompanied by a focus on marginalised experiences and refusal to foreground a single explanation for social inequalities, intersectionality offers a mindset, mood, or way of thinking that leads practitioners to do data work differently. In this sense, how we talk about intersectionality matters. In her study of equality work in UK non-governmental organisations, Christoffersen (2024, p.16) describes the existence of 'a range of definitions of intersectionality which thus leaves it underdetermined' and, when deployed in equality work contexts, intersectionality 'is largely individualized; merely descriptive; additive; and superficial'. In this final section, I explore the limits of an intersectional approach to data and, ultimately, what it is unable to deliver when it comes to addressing social inequalities in higher education.

Intersectionality fails to recognise lives beyond the expected labels

An intersectional approach to data suggests that by adopting different practices (for example, acknowledging the interconnectedness of gender and race inequalities, starting analysis by considering those *most marginalised*), researchers can uncover stories that are missed by a siloed approach to identity categories. However, even when an intersectional approach to data is adopted, it remains unclear whether the experiences of those located in non-normative identity categories are recognised. Science and technology studies scholars Geoffrey C. Bowker and Susan Leigh Star (1999, p.325) note, 'Classification systems always have other categories, to which actants (entities or people) who remain effectively invisible to the scheme are assigned'. In higher education, some categories remain situated outside the realm of *knowability*. As Raha and van der Drift (2024, p.146) observe, 'the ruse of institutions is that they only offer choices of pre-existing pathways in the institution'.

So, who ultimately decides what categories become *knowable* and are included under the banner of intersectionality? Consider the approach of HESA (2025), which requires the sex data of higher education staff to be recorded as either 'male' or 'female', unless the staff member is from outside the UK and 'has a legal sex other than male or female'. For example, a third category of '*divers*' has had legal recognition in Germany since 2018. The rules that determine the identity options available to staff in higher education circumscribe the potential of an intersectional approach as this approach can only engage what is understood as *knowable*.

Related to this critique, scholar Judith A. Clair and colleagues (2019) contrast experiences of marginalisation that a Black woman and a Black gender fluid person might encounter at work. An intersectional lens can help explain the experiences of the Black woman but something different is required to explain the experiences of the Black gender fluid person because 'marginalization results not only from the status of the group an individual belongs to but also from the degree to which the individual's identity is perceived as categorically normative' (2019, p.608). Clair et al. (2019) expand on this claim, noting that many demographic identities fall outside of existing categorical systems due to multiplicity, mobility, uncertainty, or being acategorical in nature. Similarly, scholar Marquis Bey (2023, p.342) argues how 'intersectionality often cannot account for the being of multiple things *in the same identificatory category at the same time*' (italics in original), making the point that trans women are not able to be genderqueer, nonbinary, and 'men' all at the same time.

The problematic relationship between categories located outside of existing norms and an intersectional approach to data deserves further attention. In my writing on data's intersection with identity categories (Guyan, 2022, 2025), I deploy the term 'who counts' as its double meaning highlights that in order to 'count' (or be understood as 'worth counting'), you first have to be understood as human. Sojourner Truth, an African American abolitionist and civil rights campaigner who lived between 1797 and 1883, famously asked (Lewis, 2019): 'Ain't I a woman?'. More recently, several scholars – including Hortense Spillers (1987) and Patrice D. Douglass (2018) – have highlighted how the category of 'gender' is reserved for bodies understood as human; a category that has excluded Black people throughout long periods of history. As Nash (2018, p.21) explains, 'gender – as a category of analysis – fails to describe both black bodies' location as outside of the Human, and the violent force of antiblackness'.

Intersectionality makes categories more meaningful

The interlocking of identities and categories creates new configurations, which, according to tech researcher Caitlin Bentley and colleagues (2023: 4), 'are always changing and incomplete'. When an intersectional approach to data reveals insights that are more than the sum of their parts, does this approach also bring something new into existence that exists outside the dataset? As previously explored in scholarship on science and technology studies (Guyan, 2022; Law, 2009), the act of counting and measuring something changes the thing being measured. For example, writing on numerical data, Espeland and

Stevens (2008: 412) describe how 'turning qualities into quantities creates new things and new relations among things'. Relatedly, the repeated documentation of social inequalities between groups – in increasingly granular detail – can 'serve to reinforce ideas of inherent differences between groups rather than to point towards actionable solutions' (Bauer et al., 2021, p.2).

Making categories more meaningful entails risks. One high-profile critic of intersectionality, as an approach, is gender studies scholar Jasbir Puar. In her essay '"I Would Rather be a Cyborg than a Goddess": Becoming-Intersectional in Assemblage Theory' (2020), Puar notes how an intersectional approach has 'intervened in the legal and capitalist structures that demand the fixity of the rights bearing subject' but that this intervention has happened in a way that 'also reproduced the disciplinary demands of that subject formation'. Put more simply, although an intersectional approach offers an alternate account of the relationship between identity categories and social inequalities, our understanding of what counts as a (data) subject remains unchanged. Returning to the work of Bey (2023, p.338), in a cutting critique, they argue, 'intersectionality upholds many of the categories that have been bestowed, seeking primarily to revalue them rather than [...] dissolve their hold and remove their necessity'.

Puar (2020) tries to address this critique by deploying the concept of 'assemblage', which differs from an intersectional approach because assemblages 'de-privilege the human body as a discrete organic thing' and 'do not privilege bodies as human, nor as residing within a human/animal binary', with the term 'bodies' also inclusive of 'bodies of water, cities, institutions, and so on'. Whereas, according to Puar (2007, p.212), an intersectional approach presumes 'that components – race, class, gender, sexuality, nation, age, religion – are separable analytics and can thus be disassembled', in contrast, 'an assemblage is more attuned to interwoven forces that merge and dissipate time, space, and body against linearity, coherency, and permanency'.

What I am getting at here is that the solidification of identity categories – in other words, the perceived meaningfulness of concepts such as 'woman' and 'Black' – is a feature of intersectionality (Bey, 2023; Dhamoon, 2011). As Bey (2023, p.337) notes, 'work done through intersectionalist frameworks requires that one be this or that race or gender'. Organisation studies researcher Ajnesh Prasad (2012, p.569) similarly observes how researching concepts such as 'Black' and 'white' or 'man' and 'woman' can strengthen understandings of these terms 'as being stable, unproblematic and determined a priori'. Writing more broadly on categories of gender, sex, and sexuality, queer and transgender studies scholar Kadji Amin (2023) highlights how the sorting of identities into boxes (even when many options are made available) can construct truths that offer a warped account of the phenomena they are intended to represent.

Intersectionality says one thing but does something else

My final limitation relates to the doing of intersectional data work: how practitioners perceive the work they are doing, and how this work is perceived by others in higher education and beyond. Perhaps the very point of an intersectional approach to data is the *idea* of the approach? Whether or not an intersectional approach to data is meaningfully adopted in practice is perhaps secondary to the belief, among those within an organisation and those outside an organisation, that an intersectional approach has been adopted. This gap between appearance and reality builds on Ahmed's (2012, p.90) critique of diversity policies in higher education and how, in many cases, 'the point of the document can be to have a document you can point to'. When an intersectional approach to data is primarily about optics rather than action, onlookers can assume that *something* is happening when, in fact, *nothing* is happening. In some cases, the belief that *something* is happening can prevent *anything* from happening.

In this sense, an intersectional approach to data can function as a type of non-performativity. Ahmed (2012, p.195) describes how 'the term "intersectionality" can be used as a method of deflection' in conversations about race and racism, as 'when hearing about race and racism is too difficult, intersectionality can be deployed as a defense against hearing'. Similarly, Christoffersen (2024, p.17) argues that although there exist multiple ways of understanding and applying 'intersectionality', its misuse can 'further entrench inequalities, at times in insidious ways'.

An intersectional approach offers data practitioners an opportunity and vocabulary to acknowledge the failings of past practices and rebrand their work for the future: diversity data 2.0! When diversity data practices are accused of window dressing or exclusively focusing on the experiences of white women, the language of intersectionality offers a powerful rebuttal. Writing on the field of women's studies in US higher education, Nash (2018, pp.2, 4) describes how intersectionality has been 'emphatically called upon to do corrective ecological work', highlighting 'how women of color are rhetorically summoned as proof of the field's evolution' (p.4). For data practitioners, intersectionality can give the impression of doing something more innovative and more inclusive, particularly to those less familiar with its intellectual legacy. However, this impression only entails the reframing of data activities through an 'intersectional lens' rather than an overhaul of an entire system, thus keeping the diversity data show on the road just that little bit longer.

Why not stop collecting all diversity data?

If an intersectional approach fails to recognise lives beyond the expected labels, invites risks by making categories more meaningful, and says one thing but does something else, one might conclude that halting the collection, analysis, and use of diversity data is a more productive way forward. However, as a solution, an abrupt termination of *all* diversity data practices will not work as an exclusive focus on 'issues' rather than 'identities' (if this separation is even possible) invites the likelihood that activities always default to a white, masculine subject. As Christoffersen (2024, p.198) argues, 'if identities are put to one side, we are left with generic intersectionality' that is ill-equipped to respond to the pervasiveness of whiteness, which will continue to shape values and sustain racial hierarchies (also noted in Bonilla-Silva, 2012). For example, when reporting data on the experiences of women working in STEM, if the specificities of race are not explicitly mentioned then the conversation always defaults to the experiences of white women and fails to recognise the experiences of Black women.

A third way exists that avoids a binary choice between a siloed, identity-first approach to numerical data and an all-out rejection of categories. Practitioners can remain deeply sceptical about categories and categorisation, while also recognising that categories matter and will, very likely, continue to matter when navigating questions of difference and responding to social inequalities. For sociologist Leslie McCall (2005, p.1783), 'the point is not to deny the importance – both material and discursive – of categories but to focus on the process by which they are produced, experienced, reproduced, and resisted in everyday life'.

Reflections on intersectionality and data

While researching and writing this chapter, I kept returning to the question: how does an intersectional approach to data make us feel? Whether you are sharing data about yourself and your experiences, employed to do diversity data work in a university, or are exposed to data when looking through tables, graphs, or reports – how does this data make you feel? As figures including Puar (2007, 2020) and Bey (2023) observe, an intersectional approach can embed and continue problematic assumptions about the primacy of the (data) subject. Ultimately, an intersectional approach is not about the abolition of categories (nor did it ever claim to be). Rather, intersectionality can recharge the perceived usefulness of categories and keep these divisions hanging around that little bit longer. However, judging the usefulness of an intersectional approach to data according to an objective it never claimed to work towards (in other words, the abolition of categories) is unfair (Carbado, 2013). I therefore end this chapter by sharing two concluding reflections on what to consider when advancing an intersectional approach to data.

Caring about categories and changing data cultures

Tech scholar Anna Lauren Hoffmann (2021, p.2) makes the important claim that 'caring for difference is ultimately insufficient if it leaves dominant logics and structures intact'. Care – in terms of feelings of concern and interest – needs to accompany change in the cultures where data practices occur. Working on and existing in an inclusive data culture is going to help foster an intersectional approach to data. Building this culture is no easy feat, but it involves understanding that people are not data points – they are living humans with often messy, complex, and contradictory lives. The flattening of people's experiences into crude categories does a disservice to research efforts to authentically represent the world around us and the subjects we engage in our work. We have the responsibility to meet data subjects where they are in terms of how they understand themselves. Data collectors, therefore, need to foster a climate where people wish to meaningfully participate in research data collection exercises.

Material conditions and solidarity across categories

We need to ensure that data practices – the collection, analysis, and use of data – always bend back so that they impact people's material conditions. Remember, constructing a large dataset or publishing a suite of graphs and tables does not pay someone's rent, prescribe life-changing medication, or make the daily walk to campus any safer. Data, on its own, does not change the world. It is only through the use of data that we bring about change. Alliances across categories are, therefore, more important than fighting to address social inequalities experienced by just one identity category. In a 2014 interview with Ahmed (2016, p.491), philosopher Judith Butler asked what happens when we shift the question from 'Who do I want to be?' to instead consider 'What kind of life do I want to live with others?'. Raha and van der Drift (2024, p.103) further explain, 'a politics of demands, aimed at institutions, fragments collective needs by forcing them to be presented as interests and inclusion that are cut up by the lens of representation'.

In this chapter, I have presented an account of how intersectionality is applied to quantitative data practices in higher education, examining what an intersectional approach to data entails and the challenges that arise when this approach is adopted. I have highlighted how an intersectional approach requires data practitioners to understand that everything is connected, focus on marginalised experiences, and embrace complexity. As a mindset, mood, or way of thinking, an intersectional approach poses questions about subjects positioned at the heart of higher education data projects. The approach also brings into view the strained relationships between problems and remedies, intersectionality and inclusion, and social inequalities and their representation in numbers.

Ultimately, we are invited to reconsider the purpose of diversity data in higher education: who is data for and what is data expected to do? There exists a breadth and complexity of social inequalities in higher education. Considering the social implications of data practices, what hopes and dreams do we place upon quantitative data and an intersectional approach to data that, by design, are never capable of being achieved?

Reflective questions

- Who counts as a 'data subject' in your study or project? Who are they? Who is included and excluded from consideration?
- How do we address social inequalities that are not easy to quantify or translate into illustrative visualisations? How can we ensure that these inequalities are not overlooked as potential targets for action?
- Who ultimately decides what data categories become knowable (and therefore actionable)? What types of knowledge inform this process?
- How does an intersectional approach to data make you feel? Whether you are sharing data about yourself and your experiences, employed to do diversity data work in a university, or are exposed to data when looking through tables, graphs or reports – how does this data make you feel?

Notes

1. In 2021 and 2022, UK national censuses included new questions on sexual orientation and trans/gender identity, making it possible, for the first time, to calculate what proportion of the population aged 16 and over identify as LGBT+. For example, in Scotland, 4.0 per cent of the population identify as LGB+ and 0.44 per cent identify as trans (Scotland's Census, 2024).
2. Dr Kevin Guyan previously worked as a researcher at Advance HE and authored the organisation's 2021 guidance.

References

Advance HE (2021). *Guidance on the collection of diversity monitoring data*. York: Advance HE.

Advance HE (2024). *Equality in higher education: Staff statistical report*. York: Advance HE. Available at: https://www.advance-he.ac.uk/knowledge-hub/equality-higher-education-statistical-reports-2024 [Accessed 7 April 2026].

Advance HE (2025). *Guidance on the collection of diversity monitoring data*. York: Advance HE. Available at: https://www.advance-he.ac.uk/knowledge-hub/guidance-collection-diversity-monitoring-data [Accessed 7 April 2026].

Ahmed, S. (2012). *On being included: Racism and diversity in institutional life*. Durham: Duke University Press.

Ahmed, S. (2016). Interview with Judith Butler. *Sexualities*, 19(4), pp.482–492.

Amery, F. (2024). 'Gender critical' feminism as biopolitical project. Sexualities, 28(3), pp.1239–1253.

Amin, K. (2023). Taxonomically queer?: Sexology and new queer, trans, and asexual identities. *GLQ: A Journal of Lesbian and Gay Studies*, 29(1), pp.91–107.

Ayyildiz, P. and Banoglu, K. (2024). The leaky pipeline: Where 'exactly' are these leakages for women leaders in higher education? *School Leadership & Management*, 44(2), pp.120–139.

Basiri, A. and Brunsdon, C. (2022). Missing data as data. *Patterns*, 3(9).

Bauer, G.R., Churchill, S.M., Mahendran M., Walwyn, C., Lizotte, D. and Villa-Rueda, A.A. (2021). Intersectionality in quantitative research: A systematic review of its emergence and applications of theory and methods. *SSM – Population Health*, 14, p.100798.

Bauer, S. (2019). Indexing, coding, scoring: The engine room of epidemiology and its routinized techno-digestions. Somatechnics, 9(2–3), pp.223–243.

BBC News (2022). Legal challenge to Scottish census sex question thrown out. 17 February. Available at: https://www.bbc.com/news/uk-scotland-60420339 [Accessed 6 July 2025].

Beer, D. (2016). *Metric power*. London: Palgrave Macmillan.

Bentley, C., Muyoya, C., Vannini, S., Oman, S. and Jimenez, A. (2023). Intersectional approaches to data: The importance of an articulation mindset for intersectional data science. *Big Data & Society*, 10(2), p.20539517231203667.

Bey, M. (2023). Insurgent trans study: Radical trans feminism meets intersectionality. In Nash, J.C. and Pinto, S., eds. *The Routledge Companion to Intersectionalities*. Abingdon: Routledge, pp. 335–44.

Bilge, S. (2014). Whitening Intersectionality. Evanescence of Race in Intersectionality Scholarship. In *Racism and Sociology – Racism Analysis Yearbook*. Available at: https://www.academia.edu/11805835/Whitening_Intersectionality_Evanescence_of_Race_in_Intersectionality_Scholarship [Accessed 29 May 2025].

Bonilla-Silva, E. (2012). The invisible weight of whiteness: The racial grammar of everyday life in contemporary America. *Ethnic and Racial Studies*, 35(2), pp.173–194.

Bowker, G.C. and Star, S.L. (1999). *Sorting things out: Classification and its consequences*. Cambridge, MA: MIT Press.

Bowleg, L. (2012). The problem with the phrase women and minorities: Intersectionality—an important theoretical framework for public health. *American Journal of Public Health*, 102(7), pp.1267–1273.

Brown, W. (2015). *Undoing the Demos: Neoliberalism's stealth revolution*. New York: Zone Books.

Carbado, D.W. (2013). Colorblind intersectionality. *Signs*, 38(4), 811–845.

Cardiff University (2024). *Strategic equality plan 2024–2028*. 25 October. Cardiff: Cardiff University. Available at: https://www.cardiff.ac.uk/documents/2838925-strategic-equality-plan-2024-2028 [Accessed 6 July 2025].

Christoffersen, A. (2024). *The politics of intersectional practice: Representation, coalition and solidarity in UK NGOs*. Bristol: Policy Press.

Christoffersen, A. and Emejulu, A. (2023). "Diversity within": The problems with "intersectional" white feminism in practice. *Social Politics: International Studies in Gender, State & Society*, 30(2), pp.630–653.

Clair, J.A., Humberd, B.K., Rouse, E.D., and Jones, E.B. (2019) Loosening categorical thinking: Extending the terrain of theory and research on demographic identities in organizations. *Academy of Management Review*, 44(3), pp.592–617.

Collier, B. and Cowan, S. (2022). Queer conflicts, concept capture and category co-option: The importance of context in the state collection and recording of sex/gender data. *Social & Legal Studies*, 31(5), pp.746–772.
Collins, P.H. (1990). *Black feminist thought in the matrix of domination*. Boston, MA: Unwin Hyman.
Combahee River Collective (2014). A Black feminist statement. *Women's Studies Quarterly*, 42(3/4), pp.271–280.
Congdon, S. (2021) University of Bradford's Vice-Chancellor part of national 'diversity in higher education' debate. University of Bradford. Available at: https://www.bradford.ac.uk/news/archive/2021/university-of-bradfords-vice-chancellor-part-of-national-diversity-in-higher-education-debate.php [Accessed 6 July 2025].
Corner, J. (2025). Strengthening data and insights into our changing university research landscape. HEPI. Available at: https://www.hepi.ac.uk/2025/03/24/strengthening-data-and-insights-into-our-changing-university-research-landscape/ [Accessed 29 June 2025].
Crenshaw, K.W. (1989). Demarginalizing the intersection of race and sex: A Black feminist critique of antidiscrimination doctrine, feminist theory and antiracist politics. *University of Chicago Legal Forum*, 139. Available at: https://scholarship.law.columbia.edu/faculty_scholarship/3007 [Accessed 6 April 2026].
Crenshaw, K.W. (1991). Mapping the margins: Intersectionality, identity politics, and violence against women of color. *Stanford Law Review*, 43(6), pp.1241–1299.
Currah, P. (2022). *Sex is as sex does: Governing transgender identity*. New York: New York University Press.
Dhamoon, R.K. (2011). Considerations on mainstreaming intersectionality. *Political Research Quarterly*, 64(1), pp.230–243.
Douglass, P.D. (2018). Black feminist theory for the dead and dying. *Theory & Event*, 21(1), pp.106–123.
Espeland, W.N. and Stevens, M.L. (2008). A sociology of quantification. *European Journal of Sociology*, 49(3), pp.401–436.

Fabrellas, A.G. i. (2024). Addressing the leaky pipeline in academia: Strategies to attract and retain women scientists. Times Higher Education, 9 May. Available at: https://www.timeshighereducation.com/campus/addressing-leaky-pipeline-academia-strategies-attract-and-retain-women-scientists [Accessed 6 July 2025].

Grek, S., Tichenor, M., and Bandola-Gill, J. (2023). Numbers as utopia: Sustainable Development Goals and the making of quantified futures. *The British Journal of Politics and International Relations*, 26(3), pp.742–758.

Gustave, N. (2023). To tackle a problem effectively, you need to understand it. Office for Students. Available at: https://www.officeforstudents.org.uk/news-blog-and-events/blog/to-tackle-a-problem-effectively-you-need-to-understand-it/ [Accessed 29 June 2025].

Guyan, K. (2022). *Queer data: Using gender, sex and sexuality data for action*. London: Bloomsbury Academic.

Guyan, K. (2025). *Rainbow trap: Queer lives, classifications and the dangers of inclusion*. London: Bloomsbury Academic.

Guyan, K. (2026) Trans-exclusionary data activism in the UK. *Journal of Gender Studies*, pp.1–20.

Hancock, A-M (2019). Empirical intersectionality: A tale of two approaches. In Hankivsky, O. and Jordan-Zachery, J.S., eds. *The Palgrave handbook of intersectionality in public policy*. Cham: Palgrave Macmillan, pp. 95–132.

HESA (2018). Staff 2018/19 – Sexual identification. Available at: https://web.archive.org/web/20200807145535mp_/https://www.hesa.ac.uk/collection/c18025/a/sexid [Accessed 6 July 2025].

HESA (2025). Staff 2025/26 – Sexual identification. Available at: https://www.hesa.ac.uk/collection/C25025/a/SEXID [Accessed 12 April 2026].

Hoffmann, A.L. (2021). Even when you are a solution you are a problem: An uncomfortable reflection on feminist data ethics. *Global Perspectives*, 2(1).

Inclusive Data Charter (2021). *A primer on an intersectional approach to data*. Available at: https://www.data4sdgs.org/sites/default/files/file_uploads/JN_1286_IDC_KP_Primer_8pp_A4.pdf [Accessed 7 April 2026].

Keith, G. (2021). The dark side of data science. Towards Data Science. Available at: https://towardsdatascience.com/the-dark-side-of-data-science-30b554bcf946/ [Accessed 29 June 2025].

Law, J. (2009). Seeing like a survey. *Cultural Sociology*, 3(2), pp.239–256.

Lewis, J.J. (2019). Biography of Sojourner Truth, abolitionist and lecturer. ThoughtCo. Available at: https://www.thoughtco.com/sojourner-truth-biography-3530421[Accessed 7 April 2026].

McCall, L. (2005). The complexity of intersectionality. *Signs*, 30(3), pp.1771–1800.

Millward, C. (2020). Student mental health: Joining the (intersectional) dots. Office for Students. Available at: https://www.officeforstudents.org.uk/news-blog-and-events/blog/student-mental-health-joining-the-intersectional-dots/ [Accessed 6 July 2025].

Nash, J.C. (2018). *Black feminism reimagined: After intersectionality*. Durham, NC: Duke University Press.

Nielsen, M.W., Gissi, E., Heidari, S., Horton, R., Nadeau, K.C., Ngila, D., et al. (2025). Intersectional analysis for science and technology. *Nature*, 640(8058), pp.329–337.

Porter, T.M. (1995). *Trust in numbers: The pursuit of objectivity in science and public life*. Princeton, NJ: Princeton University Press.

Prasad, A. (2012). Beyond analytical dichotomies. *Human Relations*, 65(5), pp.567–595.

Puar, J.K. (2007). *Terrorist assemblages: Homonationalism in queer times*. Durham, NC: Duke University Press.

Puar, J.K. (2020). "I Would Rather be a Cyborg Than a Goddess": Becoming-intersectional in assemblage theory. In C.R. McCann, E. Ergun, and S. Kim, eds. *Feminist theory reader*. 5th ed. New York: Routledge.

Raha, N. and van der Drift, M. (2024). *Trans femme futures: Abolitionist ethics for transfeminist worlds*. London: Pluto Press.

REF 2029 (2025). Section 7 – Strategy, People, and Research Environment (SPRE) guidance. Available at: https://2029.ref.ac.uk/guidance/section-7-strategy-people-and-research-environment-guidance/ [Accessed 12 April 2026].

Rottenburg, R. and Merry, S.E. (2015). A world of indicators: The making of governmental knowledge through quantification. In Mugler, J., Rottenburg, R., Merry S.E., et al., eds. *The world of indicators: The making of governmental knowledge through quantification*. Cambridge Studies in Law and Society. Cambridge: Cambridge University Press, pp. 1–33.

Scotland's Census (2024). Sexual orientation and trans status or history. 27 June. Edinburgh: National Records of Scotland. Available at: https://www.scotlandscensus.gov.uk/2022-results/scotland-s-census-2022-sexual-orientation-and-trans-status-or-history/[Accessed 7 April 2026].

Spillers, H.J. (1987). Mama's baby, papa's maybe: An American grammar book. *Diacritics*, 17(2), pp.65–81.

Sullivan, A. (2025). Independent review of data, statistics and research on sex and gender. London: Department for Science, Innovation and Technology. Available at: https://www.gov.uk/government/publications/independent-review-of-data-statistics-and-research-on-sex-and-gender [Accessed 7 April 2026].

Tajmel, T. (2019). Pathways, intersections, and leaky pipelines: The cognitive function of metaphors for research on STEM careers. *Cultural Studies of Science Education*, 14(4), pp.1105–1113.

Topping, A. (2021). Guidance on sex question in census must be changed, High Court Rules. *The Guardian*, 9 March. Available at: http://www.theguardian.com/uk-news/2021/mar/09/guidance-on-sex-question-in-uk-census-must-be-changed-high-court-rules [Accessed 26 March 2021].

UK Supreme Court (2025). For Women Scotland v The Scottish Ministers. UKSC/2024/0042. Available at: https://supremecourt.uk/cases/judgments/uksc-2024-0042 [Accessed 14 June 2025).

UKRI (2025). Addressing under-representation and active participation. Available at: https://www.ukri.org/what-we-do/supporting-healthy-research-and-innovation-culture/equality-diversity-and-inclusion/addressing-under-representation-and-active-participation/ [Accessed 29 May 2025].

Universities UK (2022). Closing the gap: Three years on. Available at: https://www.universitiesuk.ac.uk/what-we-do/policy-and-research/publications/features/closing-gap-three-years [Accessed 29 June 2025].

Vallor, S. (2024). *The AI mirror: How to reclaim our humanity in an age of machine thinking*. New York: Oxford University Press.

Waldman, A.E. (2023). Gender data in the automated administrative state. *Columbia Law Review*, 124.

Watt, J. (2023). Reconsidering the leaky pipeline. Dementia Researcher. Available at: https://www.dementiaresearcher.nihr.ac.uk/guest-blog-reconsidering-the-leaky-pipeline/ [Accessed 29 May 2025].

Zanoni, P., Janssens, M., Benschop, Y. and Nkomo, S. (2010). Unpacking diversity, grasping inequality: Rethinking difference through critical perspectives. *Organization*, 17(1), pp.9–29.

5

Implementation, impact, and intersectionality

Arun Verma and Dave Thomas

Measuring and monitoring impact in relation to the implementation of strategies and activities concerning intersectionality requires a considerable amount of time and attention. This chapter focuses on what implementing and measuring impact of intersectionality looks like in the context of higher education. The chapter contextualises what evidence exists of evaluation and implementation research, utilising intersectionality to better understand the themes and issues in this space. The chapter continues to deconstruct frameworks in implementation science and proposes an intersectional model for implementation outcomes that can help policy makers and practitioners monitor the implementation of intersectionality in practice. The chapter then explores how to monitor and evaluate impact when implementing intersectionality, with particular guidance on proposing an intersectional lens for developing monitoring, impact, and evaluation frameworks.

Implementing intersectionality

Of the limited research exploring approaches to implementing intersectionality, much of it has utilised reflection points on complex areas of implementation research with little guidance (for example, Rodrigues et al., 2023) regarding application in health interventions (for example, Ghasemi et al., 2021) and theoretical applications of intersectionality in policy (for example, La Barbera et al., 2022), or it has been used to bridge knowledge translation theory to practice (for example, Kelly et al., 2021). There is significantly more to be done to contribute knowledge and research to the ways in which intersectionality is effectively implemented in a universal approach.

We recognise there are a variety of definitions and intentions behind implementation. We draw on definitions from the field of implementation science, which encompass the strategies and mechanisms that facilitate the uptake of evidence-based strategies into regular use. We know that the success of social and racial justice initiatives can often be considered 'artificial' (see Rollock, 2025). In some severe cases, initiatives are simply not funded (Whitehead, 2024) or sustainable beyond the end date of the project and investment. When designing for implementation outcomes of a programme, policy, or initiative with intersectionality, planning and consideration must be taken from the outset to safeguard the initiative's uptake, embedding, and success.

In this section of the chapter, we bring together Proctor et al.'s (2011) implementation outcomes framework as a tool to guide and evaluate the implementation of intersectionality in higher education. Proctor et al.'s initial framework described eight implementation outcomes from developing a taxonomy of definitions that were identified across a range of implementation research. These outcomes are: 'acceptability', 'adoption', 'appropriateness', 'costs', 'feasibility', 'fidelity', 'penetration', and 'sustainability' (see Table 5.1). Since the contribution of the implementation outcomes framework, Proctor et al. (2023) led a scoping review of implementation research supporting the identified implementation outcomes in their 2011 publication. The researchers stated that while literature has focused on outcomes of acceptability, feasibility, and appropriateness, there is a need for better evidence and measurement in achieving the outcomes to improve systems (Proctor et al., 2023).

Table 5.1: Implementation outcomes and foundational definitions

Implementation outcomes	Definition
Acceptability	The way in which an action, intervention, or initiative is accepted to the satisfaction of key stakeholders. The outcome of acceptability can refer to both the acceptability of an activity at the onset and throughout its implementation.
Adoption	This is defined as the way in which an activity, intervention, or initiative is taken up by people and can be measured by the way in which communities engage, learn, and complete an intervention.
Appropriateness	This outcome refers to the way in which an activity, intervention, or initiative is fit, relevant, and compatible for a particular context and system. Appropriateness is interconnected with acceptance, with Proctor et al. (2011, p.69) stating that there is 'a distinction because a given treatment may be perceived as appropriate but not acceptable, and vice versa. For example, a treatment might be considered a good fit for treating a given condition but its features (for example, rigid protocol) may render it unacceptable to the provider'. An important aspect to understanding the outcome of appropriateness, is that it creates opportunities to better capture and understand resistance and pushback.
Costs	It is recognised that the design, development and delivery of an activity, intervention, or initiative can lead to different costs depending on the complexity of the activity and its delivery.
Feasibility	The outcome of feasibility is conceptualised to the extent the activity, intervention, or initiative is able to be successfully implemented within a system. This outcome is distinct from 'appropriateness', because it focuses more on the particular resources, capacity, and skills to put the activity, intervention, and initiative into practice.
Fidelity	In measuring the implementation of an activity, initiative, or intervention, the outcome of fidelity measures whether the activity or intervention was delivered in the way it was designed and intended. Proctor and colleagues identified some aspects of implementation about measuring the adherence to an intervention or activity, delivery quality, engagement, or involvement with the intervention.
Penetration	This implementation outcome is about the way in which an activity or intervention is integrated or embedded within the local system and context. This impacts the way an activity is delivered across the system and the way in which it is dispersed across a system.

Table 5.1: Implementation outcomes and foundational definitions (continued)

Implementation outcomes	Definition
Sustainability	Similar to the implementation outcome of 'penetration', 'sustainability' refers to the way in which an activity and intervention is maintained within the institutional culture, policies, practices, and the system. There are three ways in which sustainability has been conceptualised in implementation research, focusing on whether an activity or intervention develops permanent funding and implements cycles of activities. The third aspect of the 'sustainability' outcome is defined as 'niche saturation (the extent to which an evidence-based intervention is integrated into all subsystems of an organization)' (Proctor et al., 2011, p.70).

Source: developed by Proctor et al. (2023)

Table 5.2: Implementation outcomes framework with an intersectionality lens

Implementation outcomes	Intersectionality in practice
Acceptability	In developing an activity, intervention, or initiative, I argue that ensuring the voices and perceptions of people and communities that experience intersecting disadvantages are centred alongside broader groups of key stakeholders. Ensuring that an activity to advance social justice is acceptable to the most marginalised intersectional communities can help the success of an activity or intervention's engagement and access.
Adoption	Centring the voices of communities experiencing intersecting inequalities for an activity, intervention, or initiative can support how the activity is taken up by those delivering it and its users. This can help in developing trust with marginalised communities and support the way in which people engage, learn, and complete an activity. This can also enable project leads and teams to think about how they can develop their racial and inequality literacy to be better informed.
Appropriateness	Interventions focused on building inclusive cultures often reaches those already bought in to advancing equality, and surfaces pushback or resistance from communities that are perhaps not bought in to advancing equality. It is important to consider that accounting for the 'appropriateness' outcome can create challenges in balancing what is appropriate to the people and communities experiencing intersecting inequalities with the fit within the context and system.

(continued)

Table 5.2: Implementation outcomes framework with an intersectionality lens (continued)

Implementation outcomes	Intersectionality in practice
Costs	In the initial implementation outcomes framework, there is a focus on the financial cost. However, in applying an intersectionality lens on this outcome, we highlight that there are multiple costs that need to be considered – for example, cost of the intervention and delivery, costs associated with enabling the participation of the most marginalised communities that experience intersecting inequalities, and the indirect costs associated with the activity, intervention, or initiative. We also recognise the cultural and racialised cost of participating in such projects, which should be factored in.
Feasibility	Looking at the outcome of feasibility with an intersectionality lens is particularly important, especially concerning resources, capacity, and skill to deliver the activity, intervention, or initiative. In particular, it is acknowledging who is delivering the activity or intervention, as individuals that lead social justice activities tend to have intersectional lived experiences, which can create an additional racial and cultural tax and burden (Johnson and Kroll, 2020; Joseph and Hirshfield, 2023).
Fidelity	Applying intersectionality to the outcome of fidelity pertains to the way in which the people and communities experiencing intersecting disadvantages are continuing to engage and are able to feed back on the delivery, quality, and involvement in the intervention as true to its conception.
Penetration	The absorption of an activity, initiative, or intervention into a system is an important aspect to delivering an intersectionality-related activity or intervention. It is important to consider how this is communicated to the intersectional communities, while acknowledging the direct and indirect impact on minoritised and marginalised groups. This means co-producing anti-racist and intersectional justice knowledges with the community to inform change.
Sustainability and scale	Proctor et al. (2011) defined the outcome of 'sustainability' in relation to specific interventions. In applying an intersectionality approach to this outcome, we argue that the ongoing sustainability of an intersectionality activity or intervention is about how it continues to receive investment, while scaling the learnings and impact to affect a more holistic transformational change for a more inclusive and diverse system.

Source: developed by Arun Verma

Implementing intersectionality requires the design, definition, development, and delivery of complex interventions that facilitate transformative action and change. Utilising and overlaying an intersectional approach with Proctor and colleagues' robust implementation outcomes framework can enable leaders, practitioners, and systems to raise the consciousness of knowing they are putting intersectionality into practice (see Table 5.2).

This framework for implementing intersectionality can be used to help develop a more sophisticated approach to activity, project, and programme discovery, definition, development, and delivery. The outcomes underpinned with intersectionality can be adapted to centre the voices of intersectional groups who are disempowered in a system or society.

Intersectionality and a framework of impact

When intersectionality was conceptualised by Crenshaw (1989), it was introduced to tackle the problem of people and communities who were overlooked and marginalised because they lived in the spaces where inequalities intersect. In giving this problem a name, Crenshaw offered a more nuanced way in which to advance justice, equality, and inclusion in institutions and society. However, while there is an exponential increase in articles and discussion on the use and utility of intersectionality in policy and practice, there is a critical need to be led by impact.

When we say 'impact' we talk about the way in which the explicit use of 'intersectionality' leads to tangible outcomes. These outcomes could include contributing knowledge and excellence to advancing equity, diversity, and inclusion; facilitating the change of systems to tackle oppressive systems in practice; and developing a more sophisticated socio-cultural and political dialogue about the landscape of equality, diversity, and inclusion locally, nationally, and globally. When searching for impact case studies and examples of intersectionality, there was little to be found articulating the impact of intersectionality in higher education. Much of the research examined the lived experiences of communities that experience intersecting inequalities (for example, Blell et al., 2022). This might be due to the fact that intersectionality is still entering mainstream thinking in policy and practice (see, for example, Dhamoon, 2011; La Barbera et al., 2022). In the evidence that was identified, authors had described the ways in which intersecting inequalities had created barriers to seeking the same opportunities, care, and help as majoritised groups (see Hallett, 2015; Kemp-Graham, 2017; Njeze et al., 2020). Research continues to highlight the need for an intersectional approach to ensure that those most intersectionally marginalised can be heard, be seen, and be part of the change. The question remains, that while we know that using an intersectional lens helps to shed light on how people experiencing multiple inequalities are uniquely marginalised in structures and organisations, how then do we design and evaluate interventions and programmes that are fully underpinned and led by intersectionality?

While intersectionality derives from the Global North, contributing author, Dave, recognises that this prism, metaphor, and theory reflects the complexity of communities across the world. It is here we position intersectionality as useful for advancing worldwide initiatives. The extent to which socially constructed characteristics intersect to shape and sustain systems, processes, and structures that promote liberty and wellbeing can also be applied to international initiatives, including that of the United Nations' Sustainable Development Goals (United Nations, 2015). The potential for intersectionality to stimulate international impact in this endeavour is unquestionable. Achieving the SDGs necessitates an intersectional and connected approach that recognises the complexity of overlapping identities, characteristics, and lived experiences within and across communities. While the SDGs address critical dimensions such as gender, disability, and age, these issues are frequently addressed in isolation, through singular policies and strategies, rather than through integrative, cross-cutting interventions. For policy and practice to be genuinely effective and impactful, it is essential that they are inclusively designed to address intersecting issues and encourage participation from a broad spectrum of stakeholders.

An instructive exemplar case of extended intersectionality and global sustainable development impact can be found in the approach adopted by the European Disability Forum (EDF),[1] which underscored the scale of gender-related disability issues on a global level. Highlighting that around 600 million women and girls live with disabilities – of whom 60 per cent are over 60 years of age and two thirds live in extreme poverty – the EDF drew attention to the lack of comprehensive advocacy organisations for this demographic. Their voices are often marginalised within both disability and women's movements. The EDF emphasised the necessity of intersectional strategies in the formulation of sustainable development policies that effectively respond to the complex social and demographic categories of individuals and communities in order to address these ongoing global challenges.

An intersectional framework for international human rights offers hope to provide enhanced safeguarding for individuals who embody a multitude of personal and socially constructed identities and characteristics. This argument acknowledges the complexities of multiple and intersecting identities while importantly addressing systemic inequalities. It occupies a pivotal role in advancing the pursuit of equality, equity, and inclusion within global human rights discourse.

The implementation of this intersectionality theory of impact requires policy, practice, and systems changes to be firmly rooted in a holistic, person-centred approach encompassing policies, strategies, and activities developed through extensive consultation and collaboration with a diverse array of key stakeholders. This process is conducted in alignment with established legal and ethical standards, ensuring a robust foundation for all endeavours towards equity and inclusion. Moreover, this framework is supported by pivotal human rights treaties that underpin efforts to promote equality and inclusivity for all individuals (for example, The Universal Declaration of Human Rights, 1948; The European Convention on Human Rights, 1950; The African Charter on Human and Peoples' Rights, 1981).

These exemplar documents establish a robust legislative standard that serves as a critical foundation for the promotion of human rights and the pursuit of equitable treatment. It is crucial to recognise the existing disparities in the actualisation of these principles in practice. More needs to happen, both conceptually and empirically, to link intersectionality and human rights together – a shift from ambition to impact. When we draw on a rights-based approach we can then better (i) realise its social and cultural impact, (ii) implement effective human rights in the promotion of greater equity, diversity and inclusion, and (iii) take an intersectional and culturally sensitive approach (Thomas and Quinlan, 2024). It is important to recognise that universities have international engagement strategies, play a role in connecting communities across the world, and have shaped international policy (see, for example, Aranguren and Magro, 2020). It is here that implementing intersectionality and creating impact cannot always be limited to local change but also within a wider global movement.

Intersectionality invites us to reconsider what impact means in each of our contexts, structures, processes, and systems. When thinking about impact for a more equitable, diverse, inclusive, socially just, and anti-racist society, intersectionality provides a framework for impact. Over the years, Arun has developed research and thinking on how to visualise intersectionality in ways that lead to clearer routes to impact. He has identified five tenets of impact (see Figure 5.1) when utilising intersectionality and discusses these in further detail in the next few sections of this chapter.

Social and cultural impact

In any work towards equality, diversity, and inclusion, social and culture change is often key to enabling meaningful inclusion to be sustained and then thrive. When defining social and cultural change, we draw on Varnum and Grossmann (2017, p.2) who wrote that:

> Though there are myriad definitions of culture (e.g., Bruner, 1990; D'Andrade, 1984; Dimaggio, 1997; Grossmann & Na, 2014; Shweder, 1991), we believe most share certain commonalities including an emphasis on shared knowledge and practices. For our purposes, we define culture as a set of ideas, beliefs, norms, attitudes, and behaviours shared by or common to a group inhabiting a geographic location.

We recognise that culture evolves and adapts over time in response to environment, space, and context. For example, 'corporate

Figure 5.1: Schematic of impact framework for intersectionality

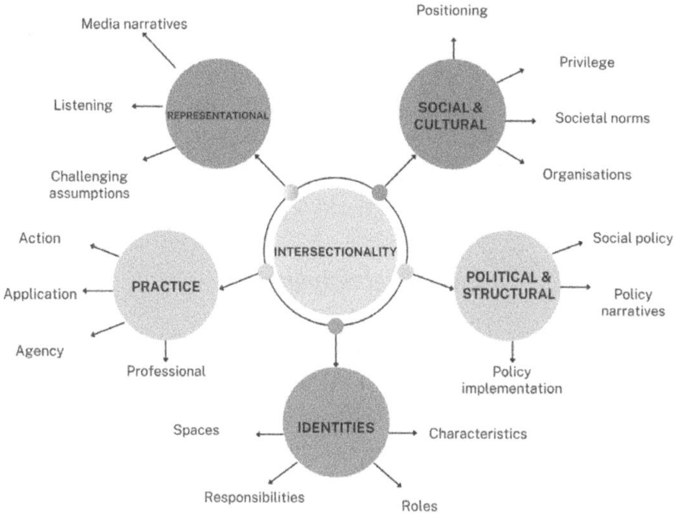

Source: developed by Arun Verma

culture' is often used to describe the commercialisation of organisations, and is named to better understand performance, innovation, and productivity (Akpa et al., 2021). When looking at culture research in the realm of social justice, equality, and inclusion, research explores the importance of developing knowledge and interventions that enable a culture shift towards preventing inequality, discrimination, and harassment (see, for example, McCarry and Jones, 2021; Mmari et al., 2023; Easterbrook and Hadden, 2020). Intersectionality has been evidenced to help encourage cultures to tackle the ways in which disadvantage is compounded (see, for example, Thomas et al., 2021; Rivas-Koehl et al., 2023; Todic et al., 2022). In terms of impact, Thomas et al. (2024, p.11) state that:

> [Intersectionality] is potentially a tool for all employers to build an inclusive and responsive culture, and to harness the talent of all employees; the counter scenario is that when institutions do not take a holistic approach to individuals who are diverse and experience

> intersectional disadvantage, then there is a loss of talent from institutions that limits the competitive edge of an organisation.

Utilising intersectionality has an explicit impact on social and cultural composition of regions, systems, and organisations, which can enable people and agents to adapt and respond to the beliefs, norms, and behaviours that effectively tackle inequality.

Political and structural intersectionality

In this section, we argue that structural and political intersectionality is deeply interlocking. Structural intersectionality refers to the ways in which structures, policies, governance, and processes create margins that censor and silence communities that experience intersecting inequalities. Evans (2022, p.987) refers to political intersectionality as:

> how the issues and interests of particular groups are marginalised within political agendas and social movements […] political intersectionality, [is] an important frame for how we think about social movement organising, specifically whose voices, bodies and accounts are marginalised or privileged within particular spaces and discourses (Luna, 2016; Tormos, 2017).

In reflecting on this definition, we highlight that both structural and political intersectionality speak to the ways in which communities who are adversely impacted by intersecting disadvantages are often misrepresented or not represented in political decision making and policy development and implementation that may have direct influence on unjust structures, policies, governance, and processes (see, for example, Roth, 2021; Arcidiacono and Manzo, 2025). A key aspect of political intersectionality is enabling higher education institutions and systems to broaden the frame on social, political, legal, and cultural contexts in order to dismantle equality silos. Delbridge et al. (2022) exemplify this in their statement:

> Political intersectionality unveils how peoples who identify with two or more subordinated groups may have conflicting political agendas (Crenshaw, 1991). For example, the agendas of feminism and anti-racism have been critiqued at length for being in opposition to each other and being spear-headed by the most privileged people within the group; white women and Black men respectively, thereby only validating part of their experiences of subordination which are not universal (Crenshaw, 1989, 1991, 1992). Meanwhile the political movements remain 'incapable of developing solutions to the compounding marginalisation of Black women … who, yet again, fall into the void between concerns about women's issues and concerns about racism' (Crenshaw, 1991, p. 1282).

It is important to recognise here that that current socio-political and legal contexts continue to narrow the framing of inequality, to exist on separate and singular tracks (see Wolters, 2024). With university structures and systems taking a siloed approach to tackling inequality, these silos inadvertently pit marginalised communities against one another. Intersectionality enables a more complex understanding of the ways in which people experience and navigate inequality in such contexts. Utilising it removes the hierarchy of inequality, or what is commonly referred to as the 'oppression Olympics' (Davis and Martínez, n.d.). It is here we know that the higher education sector reflects a microcosm of society. Universities can utilise intersectionality to better navigate the political and policy challenges facing institutions. In doing so, universities that embrace an intersectionality lens in their strategies can be better equipped to navigate uncertainty, as well as financial and innovation challenges (see, for example, Thompson, 2020; Mickey and Smith-Doerr, 2022)

Identities

Across the literature and in the contributions from authors to this book, there has been considerable discussion and exploration of intersecting identities in different contexts. This is focused particularly on striving to broaden the frame on existing identity theories (Nichols and Stahl, 2019). Much of the literature has focused on contributing knowledge to theories of identity, social identity, and categories (see, Verma, 2018; Moore, 2020; Moffitt et al., 2023). This has led to further consideration of developing data to capture more information about the complexity of communities and populations (Bentley et al., 2023; Vargas-Solar, 2022; Gunderson, 2022). An important note here is that while significant effort has been put into broadening the framing of identities and data to reflect intersectionality, this is often not connected to the social, cultural, and political systems that perpetuate and sustain inequality. It is here that those leading the change should identify ways to safely centre voices of those who are more intersectionally marginalised to be part of the decisions that impact these groups the most. It is also here that inviting the voices of those most made to feel invisible in our systems can allow for critical dialogue, and even productive disagreement, which can help support a higher education sector under sustained constraints (Holland-Batt and Jeffery, 2020).

Practice

Utilising intersectionality is about informing transformational practice and impact in tackling social injustice and inequality in systems and society. In literature, it has often been used as an analytic tool to explore the space where inequalities overlap (see, for example, Christensen and Jensen, 2012; Anthias, 2012; Denis, 2008; Erete et al., 2024). Increasingly, the research exploring the space to translate theory into practice, to help uncover processes of inequality, are identified in the same higher education systems that perpetuate such inequalities (see, for example, Al-Faham et al., 2019; Ferree, 2018; Kelly et al., 2021).

While the research highlights the value of using intersectionality to inform practice, there are still challenges in understanding how to put intersectionality into action design (Woodley and Rice, 2021). In their edited book, Woodley and Rice argue that educational activities, projects, or policy should be designed with intersectionality from the outset. In a report published by Verma et al. (2024), we sought to explore the ways to combine

Table 5.3: Design thinking and intersectionality framework

Stage	Thinking	Intersectionality lens and exemplar reflective questions
Discover	Divergent	Is the evidence underpinning the action intersectional? Does the data reflect intersectional voices, experiences, and structures? Are there opportunities to influence others to invest in the intervention?
Define	Convergent	Is the definition of the action meeting the requirements of the most intersectionally marginalised and deprived?
Develop	Divergent	Does the development of the service take into account those least seen and heard? Is it participatory and does it invite continuous engagement and access?
Deliver	Convergent	Is the delivery and implementation of the action/intervention reflective of the previous phases? Can the delivery of the action/intervention be scaled up to transfer inclusion to the wider society? What learnings can be translated to invite more of society into the action/intervention?

Source: developed by Arun Verma

intersectionality with design methodology, using the double diamond design framework (Kochanowska and Gagliardi, 2021).

The double diamond model is a framework which is premised on four stages focused on 'discovery' 'define', 'develop', and 'deliver' (British Design Council, 2015). Each stage is accompanied by two approaches, which use a process of exploring the issue in a broad sense through discovery and development (divergent thinking) and then funnelling discussions to more narrow definitions and delivery (convergent thinking) (Visscher and Fisscher, 2009). The framework uses the flexibility of the double diamond design as a clear model for putting intersectionality into practice (see Table 5.3).

Representational intersectionality and impact

Representational intersectionality refers to the ways in which social, cultural and media narratives represent people and communities that experience intersecting inequalities (Anders et al., 2023; Smrdelj and Pajnik, 2022). An example of this is the research into the 'deficit narrative' that has stemmed from educational theory (see, for example, Bak, 2001) which spoke about:

> explaining educational inequality on minoritized students and communities 'not valuing education' (Valencia, 2002), also produced funds of knowledge which call upon educators to engage and build upon the cultural knowledge of their minoritized students (Moll, Amanti, Neff, & Gonzalez, 1992)
>
> (Cabrera, 2019, p.47)

The premise of the deficit model is the emphasis on representing marginalised, particularly racialised people, in relation to only identifying deficits of minoritised groups. These representations lead to harmful perpetuation of stereotypes and embedded bias that impact the voice and participation of communities in systems, structures, and society (see, for example, Reyes and Duran, 2021). Furthermore, these harms can lead to the disempowerment and invisibility of marginalised intersectional communities, impacting their success and outcomes (Artiles, 2013).

Representation and role models play a critical role for communities to connect and visualise themselves in order to find a path and place in this world. Contributing author Arun now wants to share a story about why representation matters. When I, Arun, was speaking on a panel at Norwich Pride (Norwich Pride Official, 2022), I was the only queer person of colour on the panel speaking and standing in solidarity with my queer friends and community. The panel was a kind and joyful space, filled with individuals of all ages, backgrounds, and minds, all who wanted to be part of the conversation. After the panel had finished, a young South Asian lesbian woman came up to and told me that it was the first time she had felt seen in that city and she thanked me for being present and vulnerable. What struck me was that representation and role models had been key subjects in my doctoral research (Verma, 2021). Little did I know that I would be seen as a role model on that day. When the individual came up to me, I felt an overwhelming sense of empathy that quickly turned to joy that we connected. I did not hear from her after that date, but I often think about her and that event, and hope that she found her place in the world and that it was a place filled with joy.

Impact in this area is not solely increasing the diversity of a system, or using a 'open the floodgates' approach to enable change.

It cannot be positive discrimination in a way that gives people chances simply on the basis of who they are; that really is not a fair or equitable society. When I talk about representation, I want us to ask the difficult questions, to open up conversations about the barriers and issues intersectionally marginalised groups face, like the following:

- Why is it so much harder for Black women to become professors in our universities?
- In what year could we see a Black trans woman take up the post as head of a university institution? If your answer is not anytime soon, why and what would need to change to make this a possibility?
- How can we better link diverse and intersectional representation to the sustainability and safeguarding of universities in society?
- In what ways can we better communicate the joy, security and safety that intersectional representation brings to higher education institutions?

The evaluation and impact of intersectionality in practice is still emerging, and I propose the following template (see Table 5.4) to be used to generate case studies that will identify and build evidence of critical impact and implementation of intersectionality. Developing case studies can draw on the following to help curate an impact and evidence narrative to support the sustainability, scale, and success of a social justice activity, initiative, or intervention. For the purposes of the template, I use term 'project' to encompass an activity, initiative, programme, policy, or intervention.

Reflective questions

- What can you do to incorporate these frameworks into your programme and policy design, development, and implementation?
- In what ways could these intersectional frameworks support and guide better storytelling and communications?
- When reflecting on the areas of impact, what are the most challenging for your institution, and how might you overcome these?

Table 5.4: Intersectionality case study template

Project name	Insert the title or working title of the project using intersectionality.	
Project context	Describe the context of any system that situates the project in developing intersectionality. Consider identifying the enablers and barriers in the system that can help contextualise the implementation and impact.	
Project abstract	Outline the purpose and overarching description of the intersectionality project, its conception, description and intended outputs and outcomes.	
Design approach	**Discovery**	Outline the steps and approaches taken to discover the context and issues for the project to be launched in acknowledgement of engaging intersecting inequalities.
	Define	Describe the steps taken to define the intersectional issue which the project is seeking to tackle.
	Develop	Include details of the development process of the project, addressing an intersectional issue.
	Deliver	Present the steps taken to deliver the project, recognising the particular implementation outcomes that were more or less easily measured.
Implementation outcomes	**Acceptability** **Adoption** **Appropriateness** **Costs** **Feasibility** **Fidelity** **Penetration** **Sustainability**	The case study should build on the 'deliver' phase of the design process, and describe the evidence of the project's implementation with regards to the eight implementation outcomes.
Impact outcomes	**Social and cultural** **Political** **Identities** **Practice** **Representational**	The case study should be able to demonstrate impact against multiple impact outcomes and describe the evidence of the project's impact with regards to the five impact outcomes. The reader may wish to develop questions and indicators that fall in these areas of impact to monitor success, failure, and impact.

Source: developed by Arun Verma

Note

1 https://social.desa.un.org/sdn/intersectionality-and-working-together-to-achieve-the-sdgs

References

Aranguren, M.J. and Magro, E. (2020). How can universities contribute to regional competitiveness policymaking? *Competitiveness Review: An International Business Journal*, 30(2), pp.101–117. https://doi.org/10.1108/cr-11-2018-0071.

Akpa, V.O., Asikhia, O.U., and Nneji, N.E. (2021). Organizational culture and organizational performance: A review of literature. *International Journal of Advances in Engineering and Management*, 3(1).

Al-Faham, H., Davis, A.M., and Ernst, R. (2019). Intersectionality: From theory to practice. *Annual Review of Law and Social Science*, 15(1), pp.247–265. https://doi.org/10.1146/annurev-lawsocsci-101518-042942.

Anthias, F. (2012). Intersectional what? Social divisions, Intersectionality and levels of analysis. *Ethnicities*, 13(1), pp.3–19. https://doi.org/10.1177/1468796812463547.

Arcidiacono, D. and Manzo, C. (2025). Contingent workers and innovative digital collective action in Europe. Exploring inclusiveness through political intersectionality. *Transfer European Review of Labour and Research*, 29(3). https://doi.org/10.1177/10242589251318661.

Artiles, A.J. (2013). Untangling the racialization of disabilities. *Du Bois Review: Social Science Research on Race*, 10(2), pp.329–347. https://doi.org/10.1017/s1742058x13000271.

Bak, H.-J. (2001). Education and public attitudes toward science: Implications for the 'deficit model' of education and support for science and technology. *Social Science Quarterly*, 82(4), pp.779–795. https://doi.org/10.1111/0038-4941.00059.

Bentley, C., Muyoya, C., Vannini, S., Oman, S., and Jiménez, A. (2023). Intersectional approaches to data: The importance of an articulation mindset for intersectional data science. Big Data & Society, 10(2). https://doi.org/10.1177/20539517231203667.

Blell, M., Liu, S.S., and Verma, A. (2022). Working in unprecedented times: Intersectionality and women of color in UK higher education in and beyond the pandemic. Gender, Work & Organization, 30(2), pp.353–372. https://doi.org/10.1111/gwao.12907.

British Design Council (2015). The double diamond. Available at: https://www.designcouncil.org.uk/our-resources/the-double-diamond/ [Accessed 19 April 2025].

Cabrera, N.L. (2019). Critical race theory v. deficit models. *Equity & Excellence in Education*, 52(1), pp.1–8. https://doi.org/10.1080/10665684.2019.1630342.

Christensen, A.D. and Jensen, S.Q. (2012). Doing intersectional analysis: Methodological implications for qualitative research. *NORA – Nordic Journal of Feminist and Gender Research*, 20(2), pp.109–125. https://doi.org/10.1080/08038740.2012.673505.

Crenshaw, K.W. (1989). Demarginalizing the intersection of race and sex: A Black feminist critique of antidiscrimination doctrine, feminist theory and antiracist politics. *University of Chicago Legal Forum*, 139. Available at: https://scholarship.law.columbia.edu/faculty_scholarship/3007 [Accessed 6 April 2026].

Anders, A.D., DeVita, J., Fisher, L.A., Corr, C., and Myers, C.L. (2023). Looking back to look forward: Exploring Crenshaw's political, structural, and representational intersectionality in sport. *Cultural Studies <=> Critical Methodologies*, 24(1), pp.65–80. https://doi.org/10.1177/15327086231207825.

Davis, A. Y. and Martínez, E. (n.d.). Coalition building among people of color: A discussion with Angela Y. Davis and Elizabeth Martínez. Centre for Cultural Studies. Available at: https://culturalstudies.ucsc.edu/inscriptions/volume-7/angela-y-davis-elizabeth-martinez/[Accessed 19 April 2025].

Delbridge, R., Jovanovski, N., Skues, J., and Belski, R. (2022). Exploring the relevance of intersectionality in Australian dietetics: Issues of diversity and representation. *Sociology of Health & Illness*, 44(6). https://doi.org/10.1111/1467-9566.13471.

Denis, A. (2008). Review essay: Intersectional analysis. *International Sociology*, 23(5), pp.677–694. https://doi.org/10.1177/0268580908094468.

Dhamoon, R.K. (2011). Considerations on mainstreaming intersectionality. *Political Research Quarterly*, 64(1), pp.230–243. https://doi.org/10.1177/1065912910379227.

Easterbrook, M.J. and Hadden, I.R. (2020). Tackling educational inequalities with social psychology: Identities, contexts, and interventions. *Social Issues and Policy Review*, 15(1), pp.180–236. https://doi.org/10.1111/sipr.12070.

Erete, S., Rankin, Y.A., and Thomas, J.O. (2022). A method to the madness: Applying an intersectional analysis of structural oppression and power in HCI and design. *ACM Transactions on Computer-Human Interaction*, 30(2). https://doi.org/10.1145/3507695.

Evans, E. (2022). Political intersectionality and disability activism: Approaching and understanding difference and unity. *The Sociological Review*, 70(5), p.003802612211112. https://doi.org/10.1177/00380261221111231.

Ferree, M.M. (2018). Intersectionality as theory and practice. *Contemporary Sociology: A Journal of Reviews*, 47(2), pp.127–132. https://doi.org/10.1177/0094306118755390.

Ghasemi, E., Majdzadeh, R., Rajabi, F., Vedadhir, A., Negarandeh, R., Jamshidi, E., et al. (2021). Applying intersectionality in designing and implementing health interventions: A scoping review. *BMC Public Health*, 21(1), pp.1–13. https://doi.org/10.1186/s12889-021-11449-6.

Gunderson, M. (2022). Intersectionality in HR research: Challenges and opportunities. *International Journal of Manpower*, 44(7). https://doi.org/10.1108/ijm-04-2022-0187.

Hallett, K. (2015). Intersectionality and serious mental illness—A case study and recommendations for practice. *Women & Therapy*, 38(1–2), pp.156–174. https://doi.org/10.1080/02703149.2014.978232.

Holland-Batt, S. and Jeffery, E. (2020). Debate, discourse and productive disagreement: Interrogating the performative dimensions of authorship in the creative writing classroom. *New Writing*, 41(1), pp.1–16. https://doi.org/10.1080/14790726.2020.1788103.

Johnson, D. and Kroll, A. (2020). What makes us tolerant of administrative burden? Race, representation, and identity. *Journal of Behavioral Public Administration*, 4(1). https://doi.org/10.30636/jbpa.41.201.

Joseph, T.D. and Hirshfield, L.E. (2023). Reexamining racism, sexism, and identity taxation in the academy. *Ethnic and Racial Studies*, 46(6), pp.1–8. https://doi.org/10.1080/01419870.2022.2143719.

Kelly, C., Kasperavicius, D., Duncan, D., Etherington, C., Giangregorio, L., Presseau, J., et al. (2021). 'Doing' or 'using' intersectionality? Opportunities and challenges in incorporating intersectionality into knowledge translation theory and practice. *International Journal for Equity in Health*, 20(1), pp.1–7. https://doi.org/10.1186/s12939-021-01509-z.

Kemp-Graham, K.Y. (2017). #BlackGirlsMatter: A case study examining the intersectionality of race, gender, and school discipline. *Journal of Cases in Educational Leadership*, 21(3), pp.21–35. https://doi.org/10.1177/1555458917741171.

Kochanowska, M. and Gagliardi, W.R. (2021). The double diamond Model: In pursuit of simplicity and flexibility. In Raposo, D., Neves, J., and Silva, J., eds. *Perspectives on design II: Research, education and practice*. Cham: Springer Nature, pp.19–32. https://doi.org/10.1007/978-3-030-79879-6_2.

La Barbera, M.C., Espinosa-Fajardo, J., and Caravantes, P. (2022). Implementing intersectionality in public policies: Key factors in the Madrid City Council, Spain. *Politics & Gender*, 19(3), pp.1–28. https://doi.org/10.1017/s1743923x22000241.

McCarry, M. and Jones, C. (2021). The equality paradox: Sexual harassment and gender inequality in a UK university. *Journal of Gender Studies*, 31(8), pp.1–13. https://doi.org/10.1080/09589236.2021.2007471.

Mickey, E. L. and Smith-Doerr, L. (2022). Gender and innovation through an intersectional lens: Re-imagining academic entrepreneurship in the United States. Sociology Compass, 16(3). https://doi.org/10.1111/soc4.12964.

Mmari, K., Gayles, J., Lundgren, R., Barker, K., Austrian, K., Levtov, R., et al. (2023). Implementing interventions to address gender and power inequalities in early adolescence: Utilizing a theory of change to assess conditions for success. *Journal of Adolescent Health*, 73(1), pp.S5–S14. https://doi.org/10.1016/j.jadohealth.2022.10.032.

Moffitt, U., Katsiaficas, D., Ghavami, N., Minor, I., Padilla, D., and Onnie Rogers, L. (2023). Intersectionality and identity: A systematic review and qualitative analysis of U.S. research in psychological science. *An International Journal of Theory and Research*, 23(4), pp.1–26. https://doi.org/10.1080/15283488.2023.2223647.

Moore, A.S. (2020). Queer identity and theory intersections in mathematics education: A theoretical literature review. *Mathematics Education Research Journal*, 33(3). https://doi.org/10.1007/s13394-020-00354-7.

Nichols, S. and Stahl, G. (2019). Intersectionality in higher education research: A systematic literature review. *Higher Education Research & Development*, 38(6), pp.1255–1268. https://doi.org/10.1080/07294360.2019.1638348.

Njeze, C., Bird-Naytowhow, K., Pearl, T., and Hatala, A.R. (2020). Intersectionality of resilience: A strengths-based case study approach with Indigenous youth in an urban Canadian context. *Qualitative Health Research*, 30(13), pp.2001–2018. https://doi.org/10.1177/1049732320940702.

Norwich Pride Official (2022). Norwich Pride Question Time. YouTube. https://www.youtube.com/watch?v=3q8XzLyS1v4 [Accessed 15 February 2026].

Proctor, E., Silmere, H., Raghavan, R., Hovmand, P., Aarons, G., Bunger, A., et al. (2011). Outcomes for implementation research: Conceptual distinctions, measurement challenges, and research agenda. *Administration and Policy in Mental Health and Mental Health Services Research*, 38(2), pp.65–76. https://doi.org/10.1007/s10488-010-0319-7.

Proctor, E.K., Bunger, A.C., Lengnick-Hall, R., Gerke, D.R., Martin, J., Phillips, R., et al. (2023). Ten years of implementation outcomes research: A scoping review. *Implementation Science*, 18(1). https://doi.org/10.1186/s13012-023-01286-z.

Reyes, H.L. and Duran, A. (2021). Higher education scholars challenging deficit thinking: An analysis of research informed by community cultural wealth. *Loyola eCommons*, 6(1), pp.7–21. Available at: https://ecommons.luc.edu/jcshesa/vol6/iss1/2/ [Accessed 19 April 2025].

Rivas-Koehl, M., Rivas-Koehl, D., and Shardé McNeil Smith (2023). The temporal intersectional minority stress model: Reimagining minority stress theory. *Journal of Family Theory and Review*, 15(4). https://doi.org/10.1111/jftr.12529.

Rodrigues, I.B., Fahim, C., Garad, Y., Presseau, J., Hoens, A.M., Braimoh, J., et al. (2023). Developing the intersectionality supplemented Consolidated Framework for Implementation Research (CFIR) and tools for intersectionality considerations. *BMC Medical Research Methodology*, 23(1). https://doi.org/10.1186/s12874-023-02083-4.

Rollock, N. (2025). Nicola Rollock: Progress on racial justice and equity in higher education is "artificial." WonkHE. Available at: https://wonkhe.com/blogs/nicola-rollock-progress-on-racial-justice-and-equity-in-higher-education-is-artificial/ [Accessed 5 February 2026].

Roth, S. (2021). Intersectionality and coalitions in social movement research—A survey and outlook. *Sociology Compass*, 15(7). https://doi.org/10.1111/soc4.12885.

Smrdelj, R. and Pajnik, M. (2022). Intersectional representation in online media discourse: Reflecting anti-discrimination position in reporting on same-sex partnerships. *Gender, Technology and Development*, 26(3), pp.463–484. https://doi.org/10.1080/09718524.2022.2144100.

Thomas, C., MacMillan, C., McKinnon, M., Torabi, H., Osmond-McLeod, M., Swavley, E., et al. (2021). Seeing and overcoming the complexities of intersectionality. *Challenges*, 12(1), p.5. https://doi.org/10.3390/challe12010005.

Thomas, D.S.P. and Quinlan, K.M. (2024). Culturally sensitive curricula scales (CSCS): Roots and branches. In Thomas, D.S. and Quinlan, K.M., eds. *Culturally sensitive curricula scales*. Palgrave Studies in Race, Inequality and Social Justice in Education. Cham: Palgrave Macmillan.

Thompson, L. J. (2020). Intersectionality and business legitimacy. In Rendtorff, J.D., ed. *Handbook of business legitimacy: Responsibility, ethics and society* (Vol. 1). Switzerland: Springer Cham, pp. 1537–1552.

Todic, J., Cook, S.C., Spitzer-Shohat, S., Williams Jr, J.S., Jackson, J., and Chin, M.H. (2022). Critical theory, culture change, and achieving health equity in health care settings. *Academic Medicine*, 97(7), pp.977–988. https://doi.org/10.1097/ACM.0000000000004680.

United Nations (2015). Transforming our world: The 2030 Agenda for Sustainable Development. Available at: https://sdgs.un.org/2030agenda [Accessed 16 July 2025].

Vargas-Solar, G. (2022). Intersectional study of the gender gap in STEM through the identification of missing datasets about women: A multisided problem. *Applied Sciences*, 12(12), p.5813. https://doi.org/10.3390/app12125813.

Varnum, M.E.W. and Grossmann, I. (2017). Cultural change: The how and the why. *Perspectives on Psychological Science*, 12(6), pp.956–972. https://doi.org/10.1177/1745691617699971.

Verma, A. (2018). Intersecting identities in healthcare education: Exploring the influence of gendered environments on healthcare students' workplace learning, retention, and success [PhD Thesis] pp.65–70. Available at: https://discovery.dundee.ac.uk/ws/portalfiles/portal/28399352/Arun_Verma_s_Final_PhD_Thesis.pdf [Accessed 19 April 2025].

Verma, A. (2021). Intersecting identities in healthcare education: Exploring the influence of gendered environments on healthcare students' workplace learning, retention, and success [PhD Thesis] Discovery – the University of Dundee Research Portal. Available at: https://discovery.dundee.ac.uk/en/studentTheses/intersecting-identities-in-healthcare-education [Accessed 24 July 2025].

Verma, A., San Diego, J., Amrane Cooper, L., Harris, J., May, S., and Wade, T. (2024). Designing for worldwide inclusive cultures in higher education: Discovery report. Advance HE. Available at: https://www.advance-he.ac.uk/knowledge-hub/designing-worldwide-inclusive-cultures-higher-education [Accessed 19 April 2025].

Visscher, K. and Fisscher, O.A.M. (2009). Cycles and diamonds: How management consultants diverge and converge in organization design processes. *Creativity and Innovation Management*, 18(2), pp.121–131. https://doi.org/10.1111/j.1467-8691.2009.00520.x.

Whitehead, H. (2024). Minoritised-led charities report being refused funding because of race or ethnicity. Civil Society. https://www.civilsociety.co.uk/news/minoritised-led-charities-report-being-refused-funding-because-of-race-or-ethnicity.html [Accessed 5 February 2026].

Wolters, S. (2024). Beyond silos: An interdisciplinary analysis of intersectional discrimination from an eu perspective. In CEUR-WS. Third European Workshop on Algorithmic Fairness. Mainz, Germany: CEUR-WS. Available at: https://ceur-ws.org/Vol-3908/paper_13.pdf [Accessed 19 April 2025].

Woodley, X.M. and Rice, M.F. (2021). *Designing intersectional online education.* Abingdon: Routledge.

6

Intersectionality on the horizon

Arun Verma

There is a need to keep up the momentum in ensuring that intersectionality is not lost in theoretical spheres, but utilised in action to transform experiences, outcomes, and systems to be truly inclusive. It was important for me to find a framework we could use that would ensure that knowledge is not collecting dust on shelves, but that it leads to action and impact. In my view, while intersectionality is a powerful lens, it is also the lever to change higher education systems and engage with people's humanity. This chapter is underpinned by my hopefulness that intersectionality continues to be mainstreamed. This is particularly important when considering the current turbulence that higher education institutions are facing across the world related to financial constraints, the overprotection of free speech (sometimes even at the expense of spewing hatefulness), inaccessibility, and inequality of opportunity (to name only some of the issues). This chapter brings together a critical synthesis of arguments and possibilities to exploring and interrogating the future of intersectionality in higher education. It is here I will identify key directions for intersectionality in policy, practice and systems change, and argue the ways in which intersectionality is valuable and essential to the higher education institution's role in place, society, and for the profession of equality and inclusion.

The conception and positioning of the term 'intersectionality' has evolved to broaden the frame on equality, inclusion, and social justice from its academic legal roots (Crenshaw, 1989;

1991). Literature and evidence has grown to further develop what and how intersectionality is positioned in relation to navigating the current equality, inclusion, and social justice landscape (Bauer et al., 2021). Outside of the academic literature, intersectionality is increasingly used across the world in different sectors to social justice and law – for example, in international human rights (see UN Women Australia, 2022), policy making (see Scottish Government, 2022), the charity sector (see Media Trust and Ward, 2024), health inequalities (see Arias-Uriona and Losantos, 2023), and climate justice (see Mohamed and Mohamed, 2023).

With an ongoing scaling of intersectionality across systems and sectors around the world, I use this opportunity to ascertain how to embed the mainstreaming of intersectionality into higher education (see Sim and Bierema, 2024; Agénor, 2020; Coll-Planas et al., 2023). When looking across the academic, policy, and practice literature, I draw on the horizons framework (Sharpe et al., 2016) to contextualise what intersectionality looks like now and what it should look like in the future. The three horizons framework is used to illustrate this. I define the first horizon as reflecting the current landscape, the second horizon pertains to the turbulence in integrating a change or transformation within a university system, and the third horizon can be defined as 'the emerging pattern that will be the long-term successor to the current first horizon. It is the third horizon that becomes the set vision to embed a significant change and integration into higher education systems and the sector more widely. In drawing on this framework, I conceptualise the three horizons in looking forward to the future of intersectionality as knowledge (horizon 1), action (horizon 2), and impact (horizon 3). Higher education institutions, which are developing ways to proactively safeguard their futures, would benefit from utilising the three horizons framework alongside their institutional strategies.

In this chapter, I acknowledge that the three horizons presented intersect and follow on from one another, in that investing in developing more intersectionality knowledge will provide more evidence to integrate intersectionality, leading to more measurements of impact. These horizons would

Figure 6.1: Visualisation of the interconnectedness of horizons

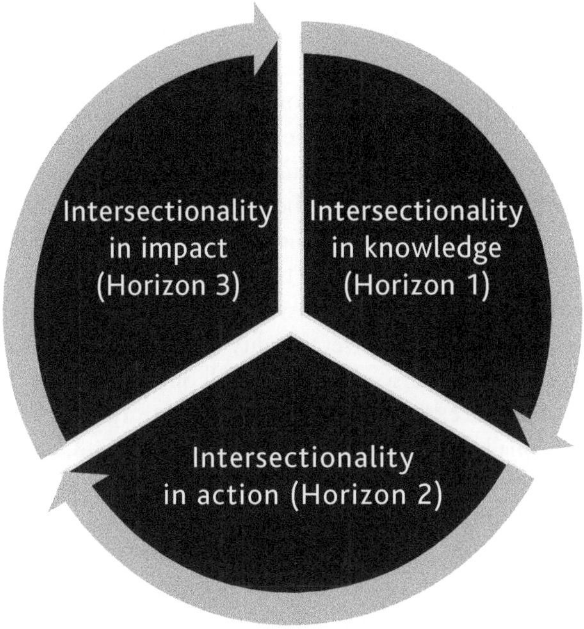

continuously improve the way in which intersectionality is mainstreamed, sustained, and utilised to generate joyful change within higher education systems, and to develop higher education institutions as explicit transformers in place and society (see Figure 6.1).

Intersectionality and knowledge (horizon 1)

In exploring the current landscape of intersectionality, there has been extensive literature focusing on developing the theory and research with some elements of emerging impact. However, when looking across the literature, I note the legacy of intersectionality from Black women scholar activists in the US (for example, Coleman, 2019) in the late 1980s. Since then, society and systems have changed over time in relation to geopolitics (see Alexander Sears, 2020; O'Brien, and Williams, 2024), technology and artificial intelligence (see Stone et al., 2022), economic crises (see

Aktar, 2021), and societal change (see Harari, 2015). With such changes accelerating, there is a need to re-position intersectionality in relation to the emerging context, while respecting its origin in higher education as a place of knowledge production.

The affirmation of intersectionality as coined by Black women scholar activists is critical. When I first came into contact with intersectionality, I was never taught about the works of Kimberlé Crenshaw, Angela Davis, and bell hooks (to name a few). I was handed a paper written by white authors and was told that they produced 'intersectionality'. This paper only served to explore how identity categories intersect. When I began exploring literature, I located 'intersectionality' within anti-racist thought and movements. Intersectionality is built on the knowledge related to centring the experiences and participation of people who are intersectionally marginalised in relation to structures, systems, and wider forces with a particular focus on gender, race, and class. What happened in this case is what is commonly known as 'whitewashing' (see Chilcott et al., 2021; Wilson et al., 2023), which often overrides the scholarship and voices of Black women. Within the higher education setting, we have a duty to protect knowledge legacy and academic integrity in how we use and safeguard the language generated by Black women and anti-racist movements. This is integral to the sustainability of contributing to this horizon.

When reflecting on the knowledge horizon, I draw on both the ontological and epistemological foundations to better contextualise the first horizon. Ontology is referred to as understanding of questions, such as: what is reality? What is being? And what is existence? (University of Warwick, 2017). I argue that intersectionality is an ontological positioning, which I refer to as the 'grandest intersectionality'. This recognises that evidence, people, society, reality, and systems are intersectional. I argue that intersectionality is a more authentic reflection of our collective experience. Enabling intersectionality as an ontology helps to address the complexity of people's intersecting identities in relation to social, cultural, political, practice, and representational discourses.

Epistemology can be defined as theoretical understanding of knowledge and how we know when we know things (University of Sheffield, 2024). When employing intersectionality as an epistemology, we can better uncover the dynamics of the ways in which power and oppression manifest themselves (see Moradi and Grzanka, 2017; Labelle, 2019; Else-Quest and Hyde, 2016). Warner et al., (2016), in their article, highlight that the epistemological positioning of intersectionality lends itself to acknowledging the complexity in making sense of there being multiple realities. These realities are socially constructed experiences, exposing structural inequality, and disrupting dominant streams of knowledge production. It is in this space that intersectionality is an epistemological tool that exposes injustice in structures, political narratives, and representation.

Higher education spaces are crucial for producing knowledge (Shahjahan et al., 2021), and 'universities have always played a significant role in the development of society' (Moscardini et al., 2020, p.812,). Higher education is key to sustaining and advancing the knowledge horizon, which can lead to action and impact. When building on the current knowledge landscape, there is a need to develop the argument for intersectionality, both as ontology and epistemology, to strengthen its position as critical to knowledge inquiry and production.

The intersectional knowledge horizon emphasises the way in which the research and literature is produced so that it provides a critical mirror to socio-cultural and political change (see Collins, 2020). The ways in which intersectionality is used as a lens to contribute knowledge to current issues is highlighted in the research and evidence (see Kelly, 2021). It is in this way that utilising intersectionality as a method to uncover systemic inequalities and injustice can help ensure the mainstreaming and prioritisation of intersectionality.

In a society where resources, markets, and technological innovation are becoming increasingly saturated (see Lee and Stensaker, 2021), it is critical to explore rapidly evolving issues and pressures on the higher education system using an intersectional lens. This is to ensure we continue to challenge inequalities and oppressive practice through widening the frame on our understanding of compounding identities in relation to structural, cultural, and political narratives (see Bastia et al., 2022; Roth, 2021). The way in which knowledge is produced and mainstreamed exacerbates polarised views in systems and society (see Piterman, 2021; Martella and Pavan, 2023). In particular, within the media, social and political narratives are positioned as dualisms, such as 'us vs. them,' 'left vs. right,' 'him vs. her,' 'her vs. them' (see Kaplan, 2020). When we use knowledge to uphold such dualisms, we increasingly contribute knowledge that directly and inadvertently separates communities (see Gohrisch, 2023; Gohrisch and Stedman, 2023). In doing so, we continue to create knowledge in silos rather than promoting interdisciplinarity, collegiality, and connectedness (see Popęda, 2025).

There is a pressing challenge of polarisation in higher education, which reflects wider patterns in society. Issue pertaining to freedom of speech (see Adler and Drieschova, 2021), transgender rights (see Tudor, 2021), hybrid working (see Khatun et al., 2024), and even student protest (see Ntombana et al., 2023) are particularly polarised. These are some exemplar issues that have been represented by society and the media as two single tracks in competition with one another (see Lee and Tipoe, 2024). If we take the example of freedom of speech and equalities in higher education, we have seen two single track narratives presented. The first track refers to those that perceive freedom of speech to be under threat from advancing equality, and the second track point out that equality supports freedom of speech. If we are contributing intersectional knowledge on this horizon, we would direct knowledge production to where the two tracks overlap, centring those experiencing intersectional oppression, to develop a clearer pathway to maintaining and progressing our collective civil liberties and free expression (see Suyahman et al., 2025; Blell et al., 2022). Using intersectionality to challenge regressive dualisms of understanding and knowledge can help us continue to embrace the ways in which achieving equality celebrates our intersecting differences and moves society to a more joyful place (Luna et al., 2024; Curington et al., 2024). When we continue to add to this knowledge horizon, we have a strong opportunity to dismantle societal polarisation and build good relations (see Place, 2022).

Intersectionality in action (horizon 2)

The second horizon is the emphasis building on the knowledge horizon to inform the development and design of intersectionality actions, initiatives, programmes, and policies in higher education.

The action horizon directly addresses the need for more case studies, evidence, and examples of where and how intersectionality is put into action. During my keynote at a national equality, diversity, and inclusion conference (Advance HE, n.d.), I described identifying thousands of Google Scholar results, searching for literature by using the word 'intersectionality' in the title and/or abstract of literature, and argued that in order to accelerate intersectionality into action, there needs to be more practice sharing to enable higher education stakeholders to action intersectionality. When thinking about putting intersectionality into action, I identify three levels of action for intersectionality, referring to macro, meso, and micro levels. (see Harden et al., 2020; Stets, 2021).

Macro-level

This level of action occurs at a system, national, or global scale. These can be actions and changes that are developed with higher education stakeholders and systems of power to intervene at a level that enables accountability and transparency towards a constructive disruption of oppression and marginalisation. These may look like national and institutional strategies. The intersectionality action at a macro-level would focus on developing systems-level strategies, drawing on the impact and implementation framework of intersectionality. It would ensure that the people and communities who experience intersecting inequalities are centred in these strategies and actions to help achieve more inclusive and socially just systems. The macro actions are ones which require those with responsibility and power to champion intersectionality and social justice in order to affect a systems change. It is often the visible role-modelling and rhetoric used at a macro-level that can help navigate resistance. A good example of such practices are institutional equalities frameworks, which seek to take a whole-systems approach to change (se Foster, 2025). A macro-level action might be the championing of one institution, or the entire sector coming together to tackle inequality.

Meso-level

Actions at this level are focused on the spaces between the macro- and micro-level that support and enable intersectionality to bridge the gap between higher education policy and practice. The meso-level is where intersectionality actions might be situated, ensuring that the university communities that experience intersecting inequalities are influencing the actions and interventions to promote connectivity between the macro- and micro-levels. When reflecting on the meso-level, I refer to the ways in which we create connections between 'what is being said' and 'what is being done' at a macro-level and how it impacts the micro-level. It is this liminal space where transformative action happens. I have worked across multiple sectors and industries and the place in which transformative cultures can often run into issues is at this meso-level. An example of this was when I was at an institution and my colleagues described the middle section, or middle managers, of a system or society as the 'permafrost', leading to productivity, innovation, and growth often being disempowered and disabled. This is not necessarily the fault of the middle sections or middle managers. This is a product of a hierarchical system that can disarm and disable the agency of middle managers in putting intersectionality into practice (see Long et al., 2025). Meso-level actions should find ways to thaw the permafrost and to help people recognise their roles and responsibilities in championing macro-level initiatives. It is possible here that intersectionality can shed light on new organisational higher education structures that are more inclusive, distribute leadership and accountability more liberally, and reflect the global intersectional community of students and staff that fill our universities' digital and physical campuses.

Micro-level

It is at the micro-level where actions are focused to empower people and communities, contextualised by the immediate higher education context and environment. These might be interventions that focus on social, behavioural, and cultural capability. This level focuses on interventions that work to empower communities experiencing intersecting disadvantages, challenges norms that perpetuate a deficit narrative of marginalised communities, and promotes wider community and public participation and engagement, which can be truly transformative for people.

It is the micro-level interactions where racism and intersectional oppression are disempowering and cause harm. While we might refer to these acts as micro-aggressions, I continue to argue that there can be no such thing as a micro-aggression, because the impact it can have on an individual almost always leads to debilitating and traumatic outcomes (see Thompson and Dale, 2021). It is important to recognise the power of this everyday oppression. I remember experiencing intersectional injustices on a number of occasions that compounded over time. In social settings, I was often racialised and fetishised by white gay men as 'exotic'; they saw me only as the brown skin to be used. Later on in life, I was labelled 'corner shop' which was disguised as 'banter' and met with humiliating laughter. The abuse was not just in the queer spaces; in my professional environment, senior academics told me that I need to 'tone it down' referring to my gay identity. This everyday oppression was insidious to my everyday existence. It may have seemed insignificant to those that directed their aggression towards me, but these were the small hits that happened repeatedly over months and years when I was in higher education institutions. I hadn't realised the impact of these words, until I continuously found myself anxious, nervous, and sad. The experience of receiving such aggressions led to me being fearful of forming friendships and relationships within higher education LGBTQIA+ networks and being in queer venues. Developing micro-actions at this level to proactively change the trajectory of the way in which intersectionally marginalised communities experience systems and society should both tackle the contextual issues and support the individuals who live with such trauma.

Actions can also be premised on enabling physical environments to be more inclusive and intersectional. I have connected and collaborated with many universities in the world, and I have not yet seen a permanent space in universities that celebrates the contributions of racialised women of colour (see Knight, 2020; Ziaee, 2024). These micro-actions to create more intersectional spaces can bring joyful and constructive disruption to spaces that have previously not allowed liberal thinking and creative dialogue. Micro-actions can simply be developed through inclusive signage, diversifying portraits, and modernising ways to celebrate new knowledge and enterprise. There are ways in which actions, interventions, and programmes can be developed to put intersectionality into action (see Table 6.1).

Intersectionality and impact (horizon 3)

When developing more sophisticated evidence and knowledge about intersectionality, leading to more examples of action and practice, it is important to consider approaches and methods to measuring and evaluating the impact of intersectionality knowledge and action.

One of the ways in which we can collectively articulate a roadmap to putting intersectionality into action and measuring the impact is by using a theory of change framework (see Wendt, 2021; Jankvist et al., 2021). The Center for Theory of Change (2023, para 1) states that:

> Theory of Change is essentially a comprehensive description and illustration of how and why a desired change is expected to happen in a particular context. It is focused in particular on mapping out or 'filling in' what has been described as the 'missing middle' between what a program or change initiative does (its activities or interventions) and how these lead to desired goals being achieved. It does this by first identifying the desired long-term goals and then works back from these to identify all the conditions (outcomes) that must be in place (and how these related to one another causally) for the goals to occur.

Theory of change frameworks have been utilised to help address social injustice (see Klugman, 2023), enable participatory justice and action (see Bello-Bravo et al., 2022), harness culturally responsive interventions (see Meyer et al., 2021) and even underpinned by an intersectionality lens (see Davis et al., 2024; Gadsden et al., 2024; Svihla et al., 2023). In this section, I outline what a theory of change framework looks like for putting intersectionality into action in the higher education context. The Government Analysis Function (n.d.) developed an 11-step approach to developing a theory of change for generating social

Table 6.1: Examples of different macro-, meso-, and micro-actions through an intersectionality lens

Level	Exemplar actions	Intersectionality reflections
Macro	- National policy development and implementation - Political advocacy and influencing - Sector wide strategy development and implementation - Institutional strategy development and implementation	Think about the ways in which intersectionality is surfaced and centred in social policy design, development, and strategy development. In order to put actions and interventions into place here, the capacity and skill of systems leaders need to be developed to be able to engage with the most intersectionally marginalised. Work with experts to enable those least seen, heard, and able to participate in the changes that impact them the most.
Meso	- Programme strategy, design, and delivery - Policy to practice initiatives - Continuous improvement cycle development - Cultural interventions	Putting intersectionality into action at this level is to create forums, spaces, and learning opportunities for those intersectionally underrepresented to be able to engage with changes and decision making at the macro-level. It is where research interventions may be conducted to better understand inter-level cultures that can help strengthen the fidelity of macro-actions at the micro-level. This can be the space in which intersectional cultures are better understood and can reflect on the impact and implementation framework detailed in the previous chapter.
Micro	- Behavioural change programmes - Learning programmes - Self-directed change activities - Contextual and environmental change actions	The actions at this level should be about using the conceptualisation of intersectionality as a key principle and value in what is being designed and delivered. Create opportunities for deep learning with what intersectionality is; how intersecting inequalities manifest themselves at the micro-, meso- and macro-levels; and equip communities with the skills to proactively tackle intersectional injustice.

impact, comprising of the following: (1) stakeholder engagement, (2) evidence review, (3) setting the impact statement, (4) defining outcomes, (5) identifying outputs and activities, (6) inputs, (7) assumptions, (8) acknowledging the risks, (9) applying causal risks, (10) producing the schematic, and (11) cultivating a monitoring and evaluation plan.

This section of the chapter presents a theory of change for intersectionality to assist in monitoring and evaluating that a change has happened as a result of putting intersectionality into action for this horizon.

Stakeholder engagement and participation

The stakeholder engagement step of the theory of change approach requires a clear evidence base of engaging communities who are intersectionally underrepresented and disadvantaged. It requires the team leading the action to outline the steps taken to engage a diverse group of stakeholders. Teams should consider how they are using an appreciative, strengths-based, and culturally sensitive approach to engaging diverse stakeholders (see Kapilashrami et al., 2023; Osobajo et al., 2023). Stakeholder engagement requires systems to authentically engage with 'invisible' stakeholders, to make concerted efforts towards sustainable relationships and trust with intersectionally marginalised communities. Building relationships and trust with communities can only work when approaches to systems change move from consultation (typically conducted at specific points of the change-making process), to a more participatory approach (the continuous engagement and empowerment of communities to shape and influence change). Focusing on participatory action can lead to developing deep solutions that build faith between communities and systems, while achieving a sense of involvement in decisions that will impact society and liberty the most (Fursova et al., 2022; Thomas and Macnab, 2019).

There is an incredible mantra, often stated in times of social justice activism, that says, 'nothing about us, without us' (see Kaufmann, 2022). I was working for an organisation at the time when there were volatile protests and campaigns surrounding the discussions of trans rights, gender, and sex. A person in power decided to host a discussion on these issues without ensuring the platform and space were safe and balanced, and excluded any representation from the trans community. The event proceeded to centre the voice of only one person on one side of the argument, rather than creating a balanced space for critical and dignified inquiry. While this event happened, I was contacted by countless peers from the queer, trans, and non-binary community requesting accountability for why those living at those intersections of inequality could not have been represented, seen, or heard.

At a follow-up boardroom-style meeting, a large group of us were convened to share our reflections on this event. I'm not sure if you have ever had this similar feeling of when you are in a meeting, and what you are hearing is so peculiar, you feel your gut start to bubble, you feel tension in your muscles, you feel your heart racing and your mind trying to rehearse what you want to say in a way that is coherent, diplomatic and emotionally palatable.

Well, in this moment the bubbles got to me, and I soon realised I was speaking truth to power. I articulated my feelings, and I expressed my view that this event should never have happened out of respect for the principle 'nothing about us without us'. My bravery was perhaps possible because I was working the end of my notice, and I was sincerely tired of hearing words without meaningfully trying to find ways to build connections and trust with those marginalised at the intersections of inequalities. It is vital we strive to include the voices of those most intersectionally marginalised in the stakeholder engagement and participation phase, and stop making decisions *for* people but instead *with* them.

Evidence gathering and review

Exploring and gathering evidence is key to better understanding the context in which the action, intervention, or initiative is being put into place. This can mean ensuring the presence of authors from diverse global regions – for example, centring Global Majority and Global South knowledges to better inform and understand the structural and socio-cultural context of intersectionality action (Raval et al., 2024; Marfo, 2024). Taking a proportionate and balanced approach to evidence gathering can help ensure a more intricate evaluation of the impact of the intersectionality action. The notion of an intersectional dataset to better understand systems is often used to try and capture the intersecting identities and characteristics on a dashboard that can describe the complexity of people in a system and society (Gould et al., 2023). As reflected in Chapter Four of this volume, 'An Intersectional Approach to Data', data should not end by disaggregating it to a granular level. Intersectional data should be situated within the structure and be scrutinised to explore why minoritised communities are where they are in the system and what routes to success these communities might have.

Impact statement

The impact statement is one of the most important aspects of a theory of change; it is the statement and caption that people will remember should also generate a feeling of joy. It is this feeling that helps people commit to the change that intersectionality is trying to achieve. Taking an intersectional approach to stakeholder engagement and evidence gathering will ensure that an inclusive and socially just impact statement can be created. The impact statement should use the term 'intersectional' to ensure it is clear that the approach utilised intersectionality. This can also make it easy for stakeholders to search and find the activity and intervention when it is published. A good evidence-informed impact statement for social justice brings together the diverse voices of intersectional stakeholders' groups. The impact statement is critical in enabling communities to champion the route to change and transformation (Dhlamini, 2025). It could be that a good theory of change for implementing intersectionality should use the word intersectionality. However, using the word should be backed up by demonstrating that intersectionality has been considered and thought of in all parts and components of the theory of change. The impact statement should comprise of three core elements, including: centring the community who are intersectionally oppressed; defining the programme, project, or initiative; and identifying an opportunity to scale up the learnings and insights to foster a more inclusive community and system for all.

Defining outcomes

The outcomes are the step before achieving impact and can often provide an indication of impact by identifying the desired changes in 'behaviour, wellbeing, attitudes, skills, and abilities' (Government Analysis Function, n.d.). While it is recommended that outcomes use a Specific, Measurable, Achievable, Realistic and Time-bound (SMART) framework (Bjerke and Renger, 2017), I highlight that the Subjective, Participatory, Interpreted, Communicable/Cross-checked/Compared, Empowering, and Diverse/Disaggregated (SPICED) model (UNICEF, 2023; Mellado, 2024) can also support ways in which we measure impact when implementing intersectionality into higher education. There is little evidence to be found utilising the SPICED framework, and I note that a combination of SMART and SPICED outcomes can help produce more meaningful measurements of impact for integrating intersectionality.

A SMART intersectional outcome would be specific to the intersectional community, measurable using intersectional data, achievable, realistic, and timebound in line with the expectations of those who experience intersectional inequality. When developing SPICED objectives, it is useful to recognise the value of differing lived experiences as subjective; enable participation of intersectional communities; interpret and communicate evidence in a way that is acceptable, appropriate, and empowering to those impacted by intersectional inequality; and ensure that messaging, learnings, and insights are cascaded to diverse groups. Using a combination of these frameworks can ensure that outcomes are evidenced by both quantitative and qualitative outputs that demonstrate impact and change.

Outputs and activities

When working back from the impact statement and outcomes, there needs to be consideration to understanding of what outputs and activities will help produce the desired SMART and SPICED outcomes. Outputs and activities could range from workshops, learning programmes, data, and reports. Collecting data from these outputs in relation to the outcomes may differ depending on the activity. For example, a workshop may produce a set of principles or action learning sets that help bring intersectionality to life; a flagship report could help promote understanding of what an organisation's landscape of inequality really is; or an event could help to build relationships with systems leaders to champion intersectionality in action. The outputs and actions should be guided by the outcomes and impact statement to ensure there is internal coherence throughout the theory of change (see Ansell et al., 2022).

Inputs

The inputs are the resources, costs, and people that are required for the outputs and activities to be delivered. While certain systems may have dedicated resources for these inputs, it is important to consider where public and community participation and constructive challenge can be invited to shape and guide the way in which activities are resourced. For example, if using external facilitators to help deliver an output or activity, there should be a focus on investing in organisations founded and led by intersectionally underrepresented groups. It is important to be mindful of the burdens of people who experience oppression.

When George Floyd and Breonna Taylor were murdered in 2020, I saw a number of colleagues from the Black community who were thrust into places and events to speak on the issue of anti-Blackness in higher education. I witnessed my friends and colleagues invited to speak at academic events, often with no support and no compensation, in order to have insight extracted from them with little care for their wellbeing. When my friends and colleagues decided to change their terms of engagement for speaking, higher education institutions shifted the goal posts and said that they didn't have the money, or that the fees were too expensive. The key issue here is the way in which labour and excellence are valued by higher education systems and what such labour is worth. Rewarding and recognising people's time and professional and/or lived experiences must be considered in higher education institutions, and it should be the norm to compensate people's expertise, time, and experience when it comes to profiling institutions in a global higher education 'market'.

Assumptions

The evidence-based and anecdotal assumptions in a theory of change help us understand the ways in which components of a theory of change are causal, for example, what inputs lead to what outputs and activities, to outcomes and impact (Mayne, 2023). I refer to assumptions as both underlying and overlaying, as inspired from Mayne's (2023) paper exploring assumptions in theory of change. The underlying assumptions can be described as the conditions or preconditions that enable an output and activity to lead to an outcome and the overarching impact. These types of assumptions are supported by an emerging and robust evidence base (see Mayne, 2023; Archibald et al., 2016). The overlaying assumptions are defined as the external, contextual, or circumstantial, and may be out of control of the theory of change but can still significantly influence success in achieving the outcome and desired impact.

Identifying and articulating the assumptions when putting intersectionality into action is important, as it is these assumptions that can shed light on people's motivations and resistance, as well as empowering or disempowering how outcomes and impact can be achieved (Mayne, 2017). It is also worth recognising that the assumptions may vary from academic staff, professional services staff, and undergraduate and postgraduate students. It is important here that assumptions centre the voices of communities most intersectionally marginalised among the wider community, as this is where assumptions can be truly tested for fit and purpose. Utilising cross-checking to enhance quality and rigour among diverse groups would offer different perspectives and strengthen the assumptions that are made in a theory of change.

Risks

From reviewing the evidence through to identifying assumptions, it is important to build up an understanding of the risks. Typically, this can be done by completing a working equity impact assessment that explores the risks and mitigations for intersectionally underrepresented groups. The risks can be attributed to the success of achieving the change itself and/or they can be related to particular components of the theory of change. Higher education institutions are still developing mature risk models for their institutions, with each institution steering through a different financial and recruitment climate. It is imperative for all universities to have a category on their risk register about equality, diversity, inclusion, and intersectionality. I have seen a number of universities develop project management structures with risk registers that show no consideration to intersectionally marginalised groups who would be impacted by choices made – and, more often than not, such marginalised groups are not permitted to be in the spaces where decisions are made. Risks should be considered through an intersectional lens in universities to encourage reflection on whose intersectional voices are heard and how are they impacted by the university's structure and wider forces.

Causal links

Articulating and operationalising the causal links stem from the steps prior and help identify the direction of what inputs, outputs, and activities lead to what outcomes and the overarching impact. It is these causal links that can help demonstrate what should be prioritised for monitoring and evaluation. Intersectionality reflects complexity in which intersectionally underrepresented groups are engaged and empowered to participate in how the relationships between components of the theory of change are directed.

Producing the schematic

Visualising the theory of change is key for communications and can take a variety of forms, with schematics ranging in complexity from use of tables through to intricate visuals. I have developed a variety of theory of change models from simple tables through to intricate flow-style visuals. The key thing to remember when developing your theory of change schematic to integrating intersectionality, is to ensure it speaks to the higher education decision makers who can use and champion it. The schematic becomes an integral tool to enhance business cases for intersectionality-informed actions and they have been used in the third sector to help generate funding. The visual should emphasise the various components of a theory of change, including the

Table 6.2: Intersectionality impact framework

Theory of change components	Social and cultural	Political and structural	Identities	Practice	Represen-tational
Assumptions					
Inputs					
Outputs and activities					
Outcomes					
Impact statement					
Evaluating impact					

inputs, outputs and activities, outcomes, and impact statement. A theory of change diagram should also include the kind of high-level assumption in relation to the systems context and scale of impact. In their chapter in the book *Systems mapping: How to build and use causal models of systems*, Barbrook-Johnson and Penn (2022) share that theory of change diagrams can help zoom out of the detail of the theory of change and can be used to illustrate the overarching logic and mapping within a specific system. An example theory of change drawing on the impact framework in the previous chapter might look like Table 6.2.

Monitoring and evaluation plan

While a key part of a theory of change is to capture the roadmap to making a change, the other goal is to develop a framework that facilitates monitoring and evaluation of a strategic programme (Jackson, 2013). It is in this framework we can better evidence the impact that is fully, partially, or not made (see Table 6.3).

Intersectionality and the three horizons

The purpose of using the horizons framework is to support growth and innovation for intersectionality over a short-, medium-, and long-term (Sharpe et al., 2016; Board of Innovation, 2019). The knowledge, action, and impact horizons

Table 6.3: Intersectionality impact evaluation framework

Theory of change components	Social and cultural	Political and structural	Identities	Practice	Represen-tational
Evaluating assumptions					
Evaluating inputs					
Evaluating outputs and activities					
Evaluating outcomes					

are interconnected. The purpose of this is to capture the ways in which contributing knowledge, action, and impact can sustain the work towards a more equitable, diverse, inclusive, and socially just higher education society. However, there are some pitfalls in futureproofing intersectionality along these horizons. In particular, there are increasing socio-political narratives contesting the use of intersectionality in different forms. It would be remis not to recognise the current culture of resistance, involving the wish to dismantle the work of equality and social justice with a view to sustaining and exacerbating division and polarisation (see Acheson, 2025; Marshall, 2025). In fact, such views have misrepresented, misused, and misunderstood intersectionality in practice and have suggested that integrating intersectionality perpetuates social hierarchies. This is untrue, when the premise of intersectionality is to dismantle racial and intersectional hierarchies in order to cultivate systems and societies that are fair, dignified, respectful, equitable, and inclusive (see Coaston, 2019).

The horizons are only sustainable if they directly address and develop strategies that help to counter narratives of divisiveness. Contributing knowledge that can help inform and direct strategies to respond and navigate resistance will be crucial to supporting communities and those experiencing intersectional oppression. This model also helps to contextualise the actions, activities, and initiatives in light of social, cultural, and political resistances. This would ensure that those leading the actions are developing creative approaches to generating communications, engagement, and participation plans that connect with the widest group possible. It could also help find ways to sustain the activities so that they become embedded into the everyday organisational and systems practices. Generating better measurement and evidence of impact, including lessons learnt on how actions and initiatives have helped overcome, address, or transform resistance, would create opportunities to cultivate stronger cultures of good relations.

References

Acheson, L. (2025). Diversity backlash: Is 'masculine energy' coming to the UK?. BBC News. 3 March. Available at: https://www.bbc.co.uk/news/articles/cm2365p3m4ko [Accessed 9 May 2025].

Adler, E. and Drieschova, A. (2021). The epistemological challenge of truth subversion to the liberal international order. *International Organization*, 75(2), pp.1–28. https://doi.org/10.1017/s0020818320000533.

Advance HE (n.d.). Equality, Diversity, and Inclusion Conference 2025: The sum of many parts: Embedding intersectionality in HE practice. Advance HE. Available at: https://www.advance-he.ac.uk/news-and-views/conference-explores-intersectionality-key-advancing-equality [Accessed 26 April 2025].

Agénor, M. (2020). Future directions for incorporating intersectionality into quantitative population health research. *American Journal of Public Health*, 110(6), pp.803–806. https://doi.org/10.2105/ajph.2020.305610.

Aktar, Most.A., Alam, Md.M., and Al-Amin, A.Q. (2021). Global economic crisis, energy use, CO2 emissions, and policy roadmap amid COVID-19. *Sustainable Production and Consumption*, 26, pp.770–781. https://doi.org/10.1016/j.spc.2020.12.029.

Alexander Sears, N. (2020). International politics in the age of existential threats. *Journal of Global Security Studies*, 6(3). https://doi.org/10.1093/jogss/ogaa027.

Ansell, C., Sørensen, E., and Torfing, J. (2022). Evaluating processes, outputs, and outcomes to learn and improve. In C. Ansell, E. Sørensen, and J. Torfing, eds. *Co-creation for sustainability: The UN SDGs and the power of local partnership*. Bingley: Emerald Publishing Limited, pp.151–164. https://doi.org/10.1108/978-1-80043-798-220220012.

Archibald, T., Sharrock, G., Buckley, J., and Cook, N. (2016). Assumptions, conjectures, and other miracles: The application of evaluative thinking to theory of change models in community development. *Evaluation and Program Planning*, 59, pp.119–127. https://doi.org/10.1016/j.evalprogplan.2016.05.015.

Arias-Uriona, A.M. and Losantos, M. (2023). Unveiling health inequalities through an intersectionality lens in Latin America. *International Health Policies*.

Barbrook-Johnson, P. and Penn, A.S. (2022). Theory of change diagrams. In P. Barbrook-Johnson and A.S. Penn, eds. *Systems mapping: How to build and use causal models of systems*. Switzerland: Palgrave Macmillan, pp.33–46. https://doi.org/10.1007/978-3-031-01919-7_3.

Bastia, T., Datta, K., Hujo, K., Piper, N., and Walsham, M. (2022). Reflections on intersectionality: A journey through the worlds of migration research, policy, and advocacy. *Gender, Place & Culture*, 30(3), pp.1–24. https://doi.org/10.1080/0966369x.2022.2126826.

Bauer, G.R., Churchill, S.M., Mahendran, M., Walwyn, C., Lizotte, D., and Villa-Rueda, A.A. (2021). Intersectionality in quantitative research: A systematic review of its emergence and applications of theory and methods. SSM – Population Health, 14(1), pp.100–798. https://doi.org/10.1016/j.ssmph.2021.100798.

Bello-Bravo, J., Medendorp, J.W., and Pittendrigh, B. (2022). Just participation or just participation? A participatory justice model for more successful theory of change design, implementation, and solution uptake. Heliyon, 8(7), p.e09808. https://doi.org/10.1016/j.heliyon.2022.e09808.

Bjerke, M.B. and Renger, R. (2017). Being smart about writing SMART objectives. *Evaluation and Program Planning*, 61(1), pp.125–127. https://doi.org/10.1016/j.evalprogplan.2016.12.009.

Blell, M., Liu, S.J.S., and Verma, A. (2022). 'A one-sided view of the world': Women of colour at the intersections of academic freedom. *The International Journal of Human Rights*, 26(10), pp.1–20. https://doi.org/10.1080/13642987.2022.2041601.

Board of Innovation (2019). What is the 3 horizons model & how can you use it? Available at: https://www.boardofinnovation.com/blog/what-is-the-3-horizons-model-how-can-you-use-it/ [Accessed 9 May 2025].

Center for Theory of Change (2023). What is theory of change? Theory of Change Community. Available at: https://www.theoryofchange.org/what-is-theory-of-change/ [Accessed 27 April 2025].

Chilcott, A., Fife, K., Lowry, J., Moran, J., Oke, A., Sexton, A., and Thethi, J. (2021). The recent history of antiracist action in the British archives sector. *The International Journal of Information, Diversity, & Inclusion*, 5(1), pp.33–59. https://doi.org/10.2307/48645294.

Coaston, J. (2019). The intersectionality wars. Vox. Available at: https://www.vox.com/the-highlight/2019/5/20/18542843/intersectionality-conservatism-law-race-gender-discrimination [Accessed 9 May 2025].

Coleman, A.L. (2019). What's intersectionality? Let these scholars explain the theory and its history. Time. Available at: https://time.com/5560575/intersectionality-theory/ [Accessed 22 April 2025].

Coll-Planas, G., del Amo, T., and Solà-Morales, R. (2023). 'From "it's not possible" to "how we can do it"'. Challenges, opportunities, and proposals to adopt intersectionality in local administration. *Public Policy and Administration*, 39(1), pp.69–86. https://doi.org/10.1177/09520767231185447.

Collins, P.H. (2020). Intersectionality as critical inquiry. In N. Naples, ed. *Companion to feminist studies.* Chichester: John Wiley & Sons Ltd., pp.105–128. https://doi.org/10.1002/9781119314967.ch7.

Crenshaw, K.W. (1989). Demarginalizing the intersection of race and sex: A Black feminist critique of antidiscrimination doctrine, feminist theory and antiracist politics. *University of Chicago Legal Forum*, 139. Available at: https://scholarship.law.columbia.edu/faculty_scholarship/3007 [Accessed 6 April 2026].

Crenshaw, K. (1991). Mapping the margins: Intersectionality, identity politics, and violence against women of color. *Stanford Law Review*, 43(6), pp.1241–1299. https://doi.org/10.2307/1229039.

Curington, C.V. (2024). Daring to feel joy. *Contexts*, 23(4), pp.20–25. https://doi.org/10.1177/15365042241293430.

Davis, S.C., Kellam, N., Sanders, J., and Svihla, V. (2024). Integrating theories of intersectional power, learning, and change to explore faculty experiences on equity-centered change projects. *Journal of Diversity in Higher Education*, 18(Suppl 1), pp.S678–S693. https://doi.org/10.1037/dhe0000601.

Dhlamini, J. (2025). Setting the strategic direction: The role of the mission, vision, values statements, and strategic leadership. *Journal of Strategy and Management*, 18(3), pp.591–615. https://doi.org/10.1108/jsma-08-2024-0193.

Else-Quest, N.M. and Hyde, J.S. (2016). Intersectionality in quantitative psychological research. *Psychology of Women Quarterly*, 40(3), pp.319–336. https://doi.org/10.1177/0361684316647953.

Foster, C. (2025). A whole university approach to mental health: Use cases for student mental health profiling. *Perspectives: Policy and Practice in Higher Education*, 30(1), 1–10. https://doi.org/10.1080/13603108.2025.2556186.

Fursova, J., Bishop-Earle, D., Hamilton, K., and Kranias, G. (2022). 'Participation—with what money and whose time?' An intersectional feminist analysis of community participation. *Community Development Journal*, 58(3). https://doi.org/10.1093/cdj/bsac025.

Gadsden, T., Hallam, L., Carcel, C., Norton, R., Woodward, M., Chappell, L., et al. (2024). Theory of change for addressing sex and gender bias, invisibility and exclusion in Australian health and medical research, policy, and practice. Health Research Policy and Systems, 22(1). https://doi.org/10.1186/s12961-024-01173-z.

Gohrisch, J. (2023). Racialised affective polarisation in the UK. In J. Gohrisch and G. Stedman, eds. *Affective polarisation*. Bristol: Bristol University Press, pp.125–141. https://doi.org/10.51952/9781529222289.ch006.

Gohrisch, J. and Stedman, G., eds. (2023). *Affective polarisation*. Bristol: Bristol University Press.

Gould, H., Farquhar, S., Greer, S., Travers, M., Ramadhar, L., Tantay, L., et al. (2023). Data for equity: Creating an antiracist, intersectional approach to data in a local health department. *Journal of Public Health Management and Practice*, 29(1), pp.11–20. https://doi.org/10.1097/PHH.0000000000001579.

Government Analysis Function (GAF) (n.d.). The theory of change process – Guidance for outcome delivery plans. Analysis Function. Available at: https://analysisfunction.civilservice.gov.uk/policy-store/the-analysis-function-theory-of-change-toolkit/ [Accessed 27 April 2025].

Harari, Y.N. (2015). *Sapiens: A brief history of mankind*. London: Vintage Books.

Harden, E., Ford, L.R., Pattie, M., and Lanier, P. (2020). Understanding organizational change management: The role of micro and macro influences. *Leadership & Organization Development Journal*, 42(1), pp.144–160. https://doi.org/10.1108/lodj-01-2020-0031.

Jackson, E.T. (2013). Interrogating the theory of change: Evaluating impact investing where it matters most. *Journal of Sustainable Finance & Investment*, 3(2), pp.95–110. https://doi.org/10.1080/20430795.2013.776257.

Jankvist, U.T., Gregersen, R.M., and Lauridsen, S.D. (2021). Illustrating the need for a 'Theory of Change' in implementation processes. *ZDM – Mathematics Education*, 53(5), pp.1047–1057. https://doi.org/10.1007/s11858-021-01238-1.

Kapilashrami, A., Razavi, D., and Majdzadeh, R. (2023). Enhancing priority-setting decision-making process through use of intersectionality for public participation. *International Journal of Health Policy and Management*, 21(12), pp.8095–8095. https://doi.org/10.34172/ijhpm.2023.8095.

Kaplan, J. (2020). Against economy–culture dualism: An argument from raced economies. *Feminist Theory*, 22(3), p.146470012097569. https://doi.org/10.1177/1464700120975699.

Kaufman, J. (2022). Mindset matters: Looking beyond Nothing About Us, Without Us towards a new horizon in business and culture. Forbes. Available at: https://www.forbes.com/sites/jonathankaufman/2022/08/12/mindset-matters-looking-beyond-nothing-about-us-without-us-towards-a-new-horizon-in-business-and-culture/ [Accessed 9 May 2025].

Khatun, A., Singh, V., and Joshi, A. (2024). Perception of employees towards learning in hybrid workplace: A study of university faculty. *The Learning Organization*, 31(6). https://doi.org/10.1108/tlo-12-2022-0163.

Kelly, C., Kasperavicius, D., Duncan, D., Etherington, C., Giangregorio, L., Presseau, J., Sibley, K.M., and Straus, S. (2021). 'Doing' or 'using' intersectionality? Opportunities and challenges in incorporating intersectionality into knowledge translation theory and practice. *International Journal for Equity in Health*, 20(1), pp.1–7. https://doi.org/10.1186/s12939-021-01509-z.

Klugman, B. (2023). 'Effective social justice advocacy: A theory of change framework for assessing progress' – reflections on the terrain since its publication in 2011. *Sexual and Reproductive Health Matters*, 31(3), pp.1–6. https://doi.org/10.1080/26410397.2023.2267199.

Knight, B. (2020). Portraits of UK black female professors – in pictures. *The Guardian*. Available at: https://www.theguardian.com/education/gallery/2020/mar/09/portraits-of-uk-black-female-professors-in-pictures [Accessed 9 May 2025].

Labelle, A. (2019). Bringing epistemology into intersectional methodology. *European Journal of Politics and Gender*, 3(3), pp.409–426. https://doi.org/10.1332/251510819x15743520497579.

Lee, I. and Tipoe, E. (2024). Education and ideological polarisation: Cross-country evidence and recommendations for higher education. *British Educational Research Journal*, 51(1), pp.369–393. https://doi.org/10.1002/berj.4081.

Lee, J.J. and Stensaker, B. (2021). Research on internationalisation and globalisation in higher education—Reflections on historical paths, current perspectives, and future possibilities. *European Journal of Education*, 56(2), pp.157–168. https://doi.org/10.1111/ejed.12448.

Long, J., Buchan, S., Simpson, F., Otaye-Ebede, L., and Dawson, J. (2025). Middle managers as barriers or enablers in tackling racial discrimination in the NHS: A qualitative research study. *medRxiv*. https://doi.org/10.1101/2025.02.27.25323018.

Luna, Z., Brown, M.C., Johnson, M.S., and Pirtle, W.N.L. (2024). On joy and war: Black feminism/intersectionality. *Annual Review of Sociology*, 50(1), pp.61–83. https://doi.org/10.1146/annurev-soc-090123-032434.

Marfo, K. (2024). Toward a globally inclusive knowledge base on adolescent development: A charge to the Majority World and a plea for epistemic and paradigmatic pluralism. *Journal of Research on Adolescence*, 34(2), pp.507–512. https://doi.org/10.1111/jora.12979.

Marshall, S. (2025). Ripple effects of US DEI backlash: What should UK universities do? HEPI. Available at: https://www.hepi.ac.uk/2025/05/08/ripple-effects-of-us-dei-backlash-what-should-uk-universities-do/ [Accessed 9 May 2025].

Martella, A. and Pavan, E. (2023). 'We hate her … and you too': Polarized intersectionality in Italy throughout changing political scenarios. *New Media & Society*, 26(12), p.146144482311607. https://doi.org/10.1177/14614448231160706.

Mayne, J. (2017). Theory of change analysis: Building robust theories of change. *Canadian Journal of Program Evaluation*, 32(2). https://doi.org/10.3138/cjpe.31122.

Mayne, J. (2023). Assumptions in theories of change. *Evaluation and Program Planning*, 98, p.102276. https://doi.org/10.1016/j.evalprogplan.2023.102276.

Media Trust and Ward, L. (2024). Why intersectionality matters for charities. Media Trust. Available at: https://mediatrust.org/resource-hub/why-intersectionality-matters-for-charities/ [Accessed 22 April 2025].

Mellado, L. (2024). Objectives SPICED: A new perspective on the measurement of social interventions. Available at: https://lauramellado.com/objectives-spiced-unicef/ [Accessed 27 April 2025].

Meyer, M.L., Louder, C.N., and Nicolas, G. (2021). Creating with, not for people: Theory of change and logic models for culturally responsive community-based intervention. *American Journal of Evaluation*, 43(3). https://doi.org/10.1177/10982140211016059.

Mohamed, N.H. and Mohamed, N. (2023). How intersectionality can mitigate the impacts of climate change. World Economic Forum. Available at: https://www.weforum.org/stories/2023/07/intersectionality-climate-change-women/ [Accessed 22 April 2025].

Moradi, B. and Grzanka, P. (2017). Using intersectionality responsibly: Toward critical epistemology, structural analysis, and social justice activism. *Journal of Counseling Psychology*, 64(5), pp.500–513. Available at: https://psycnet.apa.org/buy/2017-46640-005 [Accessed 26 April 2025].

Moscardini, A.O., Strachan, R., and Vlasova, T. (2020). The role of universities in modern society. *Studies in Higher Education*, 47(4), pp.1–19. https://doi.org/10.1080/03075079.2020.1807493.

Ntombana, L., Gwala, A., and Sibanda, F. (2023). Positioning the #FeesMustFall movement within the transformative agenda: Reflections on student protests in South Africa. *Education as Change*, 27(1). https://doi.org/10.25159/1947-9417/10870.

O'Brien, R. and Williams, M. (2024). *Global political economy*. 7th ed. London: Bloomsbury Publishing.

Osobajo, O.A., Oke, A., Ajimy, M., Otitoju, A., and Adeyanju, G.C. (2023). The role of culture in stakeholder engagement: Its implication for open innovation. *Journal of Open Innovation: Technology, Market, and Complexity*, 9(2), p.100058. https://doi.org/10.1016/j.joitmc.2023.100058.

Piterman, H. (2021). Society at the edges – populism, polarisation, and paralysis. *Socio-Analysis*, 22, pp.41–67. Available at: https://search.informit.org/doi/abs/10.3316/informit.705313879663097 [Accessed 5 May 2025].

Place, K.R. (2022). Toward a framework for listening with consideration for intersectionality: Insights from public relations professionals in borderland spaces. *Journal of Public Relations Research*, 34(1–2), pp.4–19. https://doi.org/10.1080/1062726x.2022.2057502.

Popęda, P. (2025). The inherent relationship between knowledge, communication, and organisational silos: A review of counteracting silos. *e-mentor*, 108(1), pp.82–90. Available at: https://www.ceeol.com/search/article-detail?id=1327429 [Accessed 5 May 2025].

Raval, V.V., Baiden, P., Espinosa-Hernandez, G., Magis-Weinberg, L., Nguyen, A.J., Titzmann, P.F., and Zheng, Y. (2024). Perspectives of researchers engaging in majority world research to promote diverse and global psychological science. *American Psychologist*, 79(3), 352–367. https://doi.org/10.1037/amp0001229.

Roth, S. (2021). Intersectionality and coalitions in social movement research—A survey and outlook. *Sociology Compass*, 15(7). https://doi.org/10.1111/soc4.12885.

Scottish Government (2022). What does it mean to take an intersectional approach to policymaking? Available at: https://www.gov.scot/publications/using-intersectionality-policymaking-analysis-summary-findings/pages/3/ [Accessed 22 April 2025].

Shahjahan, R.A., Estera, A.L., Surla, K.L., and Edwards, K.T. (2021). 'Decolonizing' curriculum and pedagogy: A comparative review across disciplines and global higher education contexts. Review of Educational Research, 92(1), pp.73–113. https://doi.org/10.3102/00346543211042423.

Sharpe, B., Hodgson, A., Leicester, G., Lyon, A., and Fazey, I. (2016). Three horizons: A pathways practice for transformation. *Ecology and Society*, 21(2), p.47. http://dx.doi.org/10.5751/ES-08388-210247.

Sim, E. and Bierema, L. (2024). A systematic literature review of intersectional leadership in the workplace: The landscape and framework for future leadership research and practice to challenge interlocking systems of oppression. *Journal of Leadership & Organizational Studies*, 32(1). https://doi.org/10.1177/15480518241292214.

Stets, J.E. (2021). Micro, meso, and macro processes in identity change: The 2020 Cooley-Mead Award address. *Social Psychology Quarterly*, 84(4), p.019027252110465. https://doi.org/10.1177/01902725211046563.

Stone, P., Brooks, R., Brynjolfsson, E., Calo, R., Etzioni, O., Hager, G., et al. (2022). Artificial intelligence and life in 2030: The one hundred year study on artificial intelligence. arXiv:2211.06318, p.52. Available at: https://arxiv.org/abs/2211.06318 [Accessed 22 April 2025].

Suyahman, S., Karimullah, S.S., and Syahril, Muh.A.F. (2025). Intersectionality in social justice: Unpacking the complexity of oppression. *Jambura Law Review*, 7(1), pp.275–308. https://doi.org/10.33756/jlr.v7i1.27828.

Svihla, V., Davis, S.C., and Kellam, N.N. (2023). The TRIPLE Change Framework: Merging theories of intersectional power, learning, and change to enable just, equitable, diverse, and inclusive engineering education. *Studies in Engineering Education*, 4(2), pp.38–63. https://doi.org/10.21061/see.87.

Thomas, G. and Macnab, N. (2019). Intersectionality, diversity, community, and inclusion: Untangling the knots. *International Journal of Inclusive Education*, 26(3), pp.1–18. https://doi.org/10.1080/13603116.2019.1645892.

Thompson, M. and Dale, S. K. (2021). Gendered racial microaggressions and self-silencing associated with suicidality among Black women living with HIV. *Journal of Racial and Ethnic Health Disparities*, 9, pp.748–755. https://doi.org/10.1007/s40615-021-01009-4

Tudor, A. (2021). Decolonizing trans/gender studies? TSQ: Transgender Studies Quarterly, 8(2), pp.238–256. https://doi.org/10.1215/23289252-8890523.

UN Women Australia (2022). Intersectionality explained | Our work. UN Women Australia. Available at: https://unwomen.org.au/our-work/focus-area/intersectionality-explained/ [Accessed 22 April 2025].

UNICEF (2023). SBC Disability Toolkit – Module 7: Monitoring, evaluating, and measuring. UNICEF SBC. Available at: https://www.sbcguidance.org/do/sbc-disability-toolkit-module-7-monitoring-evaluating-and-measuring [Accessed 27 April 2025].

University Of Sheffield (2024). Epistemology. University of Sheffield School of History, Philosophy and Digital Humanities. Available at: https://www.sheffield.ac.uk/hpdh/research/philosophy/themes/epistemology [Accessed 22 April 2025].

University of Warwick (2017). Ontology. University of Warwick Education Studies. Available at: https://warwick.ac.uk/fac/soc/ces/research/current/socialtheory/maps/ology/ [Accessed 22 April 2025].

Warner, L.R., Settles, I.H., and Shields, S.A. (2016). Invited reflection: Intersectionality as an epistemological challenge to psychology. Psychology of Women Quarterly, 40(2), pp.171–176. https://doi.org/10.1177/0361684316641384.

Wendt, K., ed. (2021). *Theories of change: Change leadership tools, models and applications for investing in sustainable development.* Sustainable Finance. Switzerland: Springer Nature. https://doi.org/10.1007/978-3-030-52275-9.

Wilson, B.L., Davis, B., Anderson, B., Luke, P., Gorchow, C., and Nzomene Kahouo Foda, A.N. (2023). 'Tone it down': The whitewashing of Black women doctoral students' research and scholarship at predominately white institutions—implications for social work doctoral education. *Journal of Social Work Education*, 59(3), pp.1–16. https://doi.org/10.1080/10437797.2023.2179147.

Ziaee, A. (2024). Spaces of radical possibility: Designing for and from Intersectionality. *Trends in Higher Education*, 3(4), pp.1109–1120. https://doi.org/10.3390/higheredu3040065.

7

Keeping up the momentum of intersectionality

Arun Verma

This chapter includes my reflections and considerations regarding the strategies and tools to keep up the momentum of integrating intersectionality into higher education, reflecting on the contributions made, the analysis and actions presented in each chapter, and what this can mean for community in its most intersectional sense. The chapter will also reflect on the vehicles for ensuring we continue to integrate intersectionality into higher education systems to empower transformational change and outcomes for intersectionally marginalised staff and students. In particular, I reflect on three vehicles that can keep the momentum of intersectionality moving: community, truth, and creativity.

In the current world, I write these words with deep concern about the role of community. When I refer to the first vehicle of community, I honour the thinking of bell hooks, who spoke of communities of love, resistance, and joy. This sense of community is important now more than ever. I note the deepening concerns of a divided society, where polarising dualisms have become so distinct we appear to have lost our sense of unity, connection, and our relationships. I have often been guilty of picking up my phone and doom scrolling first thing in the morning. This scrolling allows the world's injustices to be transmitted straight into my privileged space. I see generations of people who have built leadership premised on fear, while on the other side I see people who fight for hope and liberation. I see the horrors of war and injustice that displace, harm, and scare people away from their homes. I view and listen to different news, media, and influencer channels that such individuals on opposite ends of a linear argument interrupt, ignore, and shout at one another. People argue from within the categories they feel they must maintain, whether that be as part of a political party, a protest group, or because an influencer said so. I hear these debates and negotiations across higher education and on campuses where people try to shut each other down. Something has to change in order to forge good relations. Without an intersectional approach to our university systems and campuses, we continue to delegitimise the voices of people who have fallen through the cracks of a system that we know was not always designed to include and advance everyone in society and across the world.

The higher education community is filled with a diverse array of minds and people who all form part of a community. This is a community that has been through the university system and achieved excellence. Even when students and staff leave or move on, they often remain active alumni of the higher education system. They are reminded of the role a university has played in their lives. Intersectionality has always been about creating and cultivating communities where those who are intersectionally oppressed are able to fully participate in and change their narrative of inequality into one of joy. If we are to ensure that the momentum of intersectionality remains intrinsic to helping solve inequality, then we need to continue to forge communities of storytelling and joy in order to demand more.

The second vehicle keeping the momentum of intersectionality moving is that of truth and when it comes to intersectionality and inequality, it is words, stories, and language that matter. When I think about intersectionality, I note that there are people who have attempted to change and challenge its meaning or criticise its origin story (see Boecker, 2024). Crenshaw (2025) recently said: 'if we can't tell the story about the inequality, we can't demand that it be fixed, they get that more than we do'. We must ensure that intersectionality is utilised with integrity and fidelity to its very roots. It is in this way that we can constructively disrupt silos that inhibit people's experiences, communities, and their liberation.

The question is how do we make sure we get that, and what do we do when we have it?

The vehicle of truth is intrinsic to continuing to tell the story of inequality, in a way that we can demand it be fixed. In a world where technology continues to rapidly evolve and artificial intelligence (AI) is shaping our communications and relationships, it has become harder to know what reality and truth really are. In some sense, we revisit conversations about our theory of knowing (or ontology) through an intersectional lens to perhaps decipher whose truth matters the most and the least in current systems. Higher education institutions play a critical role in knowledge production that can shape societal conversations. However, I note that knowledge production has become increasingly challenging in a world where social media, commentary, and influencers can decide what is the truth and what is not. It is those individuals who experience intersecting inequalities that can face compounding sexism, racism and many more that can inhibit their ability to tell their truth (for example, Rajani, 2021; Mishra and Chugh, 2025). Alongside more social commentary, there has been an increase of 'fact checking' organisations who serve to combat misinformation and neutrality (International Fact Checking Network, n.d.). However, even with the efforts of fact checking, the evidence points to the fact that it is those that are intersectionally marginalised, who are least heard across society.

An example from within the United Kingdom of how a dominant power presented factual inaccuracies as truth, which fuelled the riots of 2024, where misinformation targeted specifically Muslims and immigrants, or anyone who looked like they might belong to either of these two groups (Robinson et al., 2025; Boukari and Devakumar, 2024). Little to no attention, voice and consideration was given to intersectional communities who were adversely impacted by these to counter the false claims made. Given the role that universities are supposed to play in truth seeking and enabling people from across the world to participate in higher education, it was shocking to see that only a handful of universities in the United Kingdom condemned the misinformation and violence or offered sanctuary and safety to their students and staff who were threatened by these riots. I share this example for two reasons. The first is the promise of universities to be sanctuaries with our intersectional communities who can often be hit the hardest during times of danger and conflict. The second is to contextualise the ways in which the knowing of truth has become contested particularly for those who experience intersecting inequalities. When we apply an intersectional approach to broaden the frame on truth and knowledge, we invite a multiplicity of views that help us better understand and act to address inequality in our higher education institutions.

The third vehicle of intersectionality is creativity. Creativity plays a critical role in storytelling, truth, and connecting communities. In order to maintain intersectionality as a critical theory of reality and action, we need to be able to engage more people using creative practice. Creating spaces and environments that bring people together to experience joy is true to what we are striving to achieve when we put intersectionality into practice. Universities are built on creativity, with their goal often being to find ways to invent, explore, and deepen knowledge and inquiry through research, scholarship, and partnerships. Intersectionality offers a place where we can be truly creative in how we engage communities and develop meaningful interventions to narrow the gaps of inequality. An example of intersectional creativity bringing diverse communities together occurs within the space of the cinema. The cinema is a location where diverse groups of strangers sit together for hours to watch a story unfold. We hear people react, munch on their snacks, yet we all respect the story unfolding on the silver screen and maintain focus. When the movie ends, we leave and the community disperses. But for those hours, we are all brought together to watch and listen to a story. The principle here is that if it is possible to bring strangers together to engage in a collective experience of creative storytelling, then this could present one key to unlocking intersectionality in higher education – encouraging creation that builds people's experiences of humanity and connectedness.

Furthermore, it is through creativity that we can engage higher education in a conversation about intersectionality and better communicate this. The communication of successful equality work is vital to sustaining intersectionality. At a conference where I was talking about intersectionality, influencing leadership, and delivering equality with impact, I was asked a question about how to best engage our communities in higher education. I replied that we must flood our communication channels with the excellent work we are achieving in using intersectionality, as well as with our efforts to put equality, diversity, and inclusion at the heart of everything we do. It is of upmost importance that when we achieve equality, in even the smallest way, we celebrate and ensure everyone knows what we did, how we did it, why it matters, and how it has changed lives. Sharing these messages of kindness, joy, and celebration do not detract from the reality of inequality and injustice. Instead, celebration is a mark of what we have overcome. For example, a higher education institution that has closed the awarding gap or the ethnicity pay gap must share with the sector why it matters, the journey they went on, and celebrate the success of the achievement.

The vehicles of community, truth, and creativity are integral to keep intersectionality moving forward and ensure that it is embraced and utilised in a way that addresses how inequalities intersect and interlock in higher education.

Throughout this book, we have collectively highlighted the ways in which intersectionality can be put into action, through recognising its history and utilising it for developing policy, understanding data, measuring impact, and thinking about its future directions in higher education.

When starting this work, I was asked what my hope is for this book. My hope for this book is that you, the reader, are able to better understand ways in which intersectionality can be embedded within higher education institutions. It is through this understanding that I hope to see more sophisticated conversations, interventions, and transformations for a truly inclusive higher education sector; a higher education sector that has the capability to broaden the frame and to narrow the gaps that adversely marginalise the intersectionally oppressed.

As the editor, my wish is that this book leaves you with the message that intersectionality is vital to achieving our ambitions for equality and joy in higher education. When we solve this in higher education, and in wider society, the world will only benefit.

References

Bhopal, K. (2020). Confronting White privilege: The importance of intersectionality in the sociology of education. *British Journal of Sociology of Education*, 41(6), 807–816. https://doi.org/10.1080/01425692.2020.1755224.

Blell, M., Liu, S.J.S., and Verma, A. (2023). Working in unprecedented times: Intersectionality and women of color in UK higher education in and beyond the pandemic. *Gender, Work & Organization*, 30(2), 353–372.

Boecker, B. (2024). How we can unpack misconceptions about 'the buzzword' intersectionality. Women's Agenda. Available at: https://womensagenda.com.au/leadership/how-we-can-unpack-misconceptions-about-the-buzzword-intersectionality/ [Accessed 24 July 2025].

Boukari, Y. and Devakumar, D. (2024). Far-right riots in the UK: The culmination of years of rhetoric and policies. *The Lancet*, 404(10456). https://doi.org/10.1016/s0140-6736(24)01713-6.

Crenshaw, K. (2025). Kimberlé Crenshaw spoke at the Road to Justice" TIME Impact Dinner on the danger of forgetting and why remembering is central to democracy. This project was supported with funding from @policingequity. Time on Instagram. Available at: https://www.instagram.com/reel/DJ7TitGPCxa/?igsh=MWthNTk0bDBnbTB1ZQ%3D%3D [Accessed 24 July 2025].

International Fact Checking Network. (n.d.). IFCN Code of Principles. Available at: https://ifcncodeofprinciples.poynter.org/

Mishra, A. and Chugh, P. (2025). Intersectional Approach to Digital Rights. In P. Devi and A. Kaushik, eds., *The Paradoxes of Free Speech*. London: Routledge, pp.14–26. https://doi.org/10.4324/9781003541202-16.

Robinson, P., Ralph, L., and Aitken, A. (2025). Police use of X (Twitter) during the 2024 UK riots. *Police Practice and Research*, 27(1), 1–20. https://doi.org/10.1080/15614263.2025.2510376.

Verma, A. (Ed.). (2022). *Anti-racism in higher education: An action guide for change*. Bristol: Policy Press.

White Cube (2024). Tracey Emin, I followed you to the end. 19 September – 10 November 2024. Available at: https://www.whitecube.com/gallery-exhibitions/tracey-emin-bermondsey-2024 [Accessed 24 July 2025].

Index

References to figures appear in *italic* type; those in **bold** type refer to tables. References to endnotes show both the page number and the note number (54n1).

D

E

T

U

V

W